GIVE
THEM P.I.E.

OTHER BOOKS AND AUDIOBOOKS
BY ED J. PINEGAR

Press Forward Saints

Living by the Word

Your Patriarchal Blessing

Happily Ever After

Power Tools for Missionaries, Four Volumes

After Your Mission

Lengthen Your Shuffle

Series of Latter-day Commentaries, Teachings and Commentaries

Unlocking, and Who's Who—Old Testament, New Testament, Book of Mormon, and Doctrine and Covenants

The Temple: Gaining Knowledge and Power in the House of the Lord

The Christmas Code

The Christmas List

Preparing for the Melchizedek Priesthood and My Mission

The Little Book of Gratitude

31 Days to a Better You

Fatherhood: A Calling of Love

It's Great to Be a Missionary

Living after the Manner of Happiness

Because of Him

God the Father

Experiencing a Mighty Change of Heart

GIVE THEM P.I.E.

LIFTING
OTHERS THROUGH

PRAISE
INSPIRATION
ENCOURAGEMENT

ED J. PINEGAR

Covenant

Covenant Communications, Inc.

Ed Jolley Pinegar
February 12, 1935–August 18, 2020

Table of Contents

What Is PIE?

- Praise, Inspiration, and Encouragement
- PIE Is an Expression of Charity
- A Note on Receiving PIE
- Expressing Love by the Power of the Holy Ghost
- Preparing to Be Worthy of the Holy Ghost
- Remember—Everyone Needs Love and Acceptance
- An Experiment with Eternal Rewards
- The Key to Expressing Love: The Power of the Holy Spirit and the Pure Love of Christ Working Together

Special Note

I RECEIVED AN URGENT, EARLY morning call. "Kristin," I heard the struggling yet still-strong voice on the other end of the line say. It was my dear friend, Brother Ed. "I'm in my last lap," he shared, working hard to talk between breaths. "But I have one last book. It's an important one! It's almost done, but I need your help to get it ready and published." He explained that this book would be his final message, and that he wanted—needed—to get it out into the world. "I only have a few days left, I think," he confided. He was now on hospice and knew what that meant. Of course I agreed to help, and he sent me the manuscript.

As I read, I understood completely. The beautiful message of this book epitomizes the life of Ed Pinegar. He lived his life helping others to be the very best versions of themselves through his easy and unconditional love, his heartfelt and genuine praise, and his constant lifting of everyone around him through positive encouragement and inspiration. Ed served up PIE everywhere he went! What a perfect final message of a life well lived!

Two days later, I was working on the manuscript and preparing it for publication, knowing that time was limited, when I received news that my sweet friend's mortal journey had ended. My heart was full; I knew there would be great rejoicing and grand reunions happening as this good and faithful servant returned to his heavenly home. It was especially tender to imagine his reunion with his son Cory.

If you ever want to read how people feel about someone who spends their life serving PIE to all those around him, take a look at Brother Ed's Facebook page. Here are just a few tributes posted there the week of his passing, shared with permission.

From his grandson Josh Bushnell:

> I've been hearing my grandpa's raspy and excited voice saying: Josh! Joshua! All day today. His excitement every time he greeted me and others was amazing. It wasn't lip service, it was genuine and he truly was excited every time. It made you feel like a million bucks! I will miss him and that a lot.
>
> The first scripture I ever memorized was Joshua 24:15 because of him. He'd often have me quote it in front of others especially when they didn't recognize the reference.
>
> It's been touching to see all the comments and photos shared on posts and his FB profile. I never knew a bunch of the awards he won until I read them yesterday.

Probably because he didn't care about accolades just people and making a difference. In one of his books he talked about how we should answer the question "where did you serve your mission?" his recommendation of what to say was "earth." He was always a missionary and he fulfilled his mission and personal ministry with honor. Well done Grandpa, you good and faithful servant!

From Shane Fisher, a missionary during the time Brother Pinegar was president of the Provo MTC:

Bro. Ed Pinegar passed away this morning. He is loved by many and will be missed by all. Aside from my mother, who had done her very best to teach and prepare me since the day I was born, no one made a more powerful impact on me, as a young missionary, than Bro. Ed. I was two days into my mission, living in the MTC, and I had reached the decision that the mission was not for me, that it was time to go. I left class that day, abandoning my companion, and walked alone for hours. Fortunately, I ran into Ryan Beuhring, a good friend of mine, who ditched his companion to sit with me and talk things out. Ryan suggested I should go and speak with Bro. Ed, who was the MTC President at the time. Ryan told me that no matter what the decision, after speaking with Bro. Ed, the right one would be made. I headed to Bro. Ed's office. It was now about 9pm and no way Bro. Ed should have been there, but there I was, standing outside his office door when he came strolling down the hall. He had to have known that something was wrong as I was alone, the only one in that section of the building. A smile—his smile (if you ever met him you know that smile) lit up his face and, instead of with dismay or worry, he looked at me with joy and friendship. "Do you have time to sit and talk with me?" he asked. We entered his office, sat across from one another and, before I could mutter a word, I heard him. "Do you want to give your mom a call? I think she would like to hear from you. You can use my phone." I shook my head yes and dialed the number. My mom, shocked that I had called, and I had a short, simple conversation that only she and I (and maybe just I) can recall. Upon hanging up, Bro. Ed glanced at me. "Feeling better?" he asked. I was. I told him I was. He looked at me, and this time with a look of confidence, of faith, and of strength, and with one sentence, provided me with a blessing, a blessing that would provide me with the power and the desire to serve that, before that moment, I was deeply lacking.

He then looked at me again, flashed the giant smile, and said "It's time for you to return." I can't imagine how my life would have been different, the many, many blessings I would have lost, if it were not for this great man. I had the fortune of running into him about 20 years later and, with a tear in my eye and a heart full of gratitude, I relayed the story of that night. I told him about my mission, about the lives that were touched and souls who were saved. I told him about my life and about my family. And, in his humble way, he just listened and smiled. Of course he didn't remember—why should he? But he saw in my eyes and he felt from my heart my sincerity, and he smiled, gave a little chuckle, and simply said, "The Lord is happy you served." His human understanding and life wisdom were immeasurable. He had a tremendous love for the Savior and he showed it through his service and love. Thank you, Bro. Ed. You will forever be remembered.

From Bill Freeze, a longtime friend:

Brother Ed Pinegar passed away this week—I first met Dr. Ed Pinegar in the fall of 1973. He was a local dentist in Provo and a very popular religion teacher at BYU. Linda had taken religion classes from Brother Ed and they had become good friends. When I decided to join the LDS Church in October of 1973, I ask(ed) him to participate in my baptismal service. I have always felt honored to have two great men help me enter the Lord's kingdom . . . Dr. Joseph Wood baptized me . . . and Dr. Ed Pinegar confirmed me. Fast forward to the fall of 1999. Linda and I had moved our family back to Provo from Indiana in July of 1993 and later I was asked to be a Bishop of (a) BYU singles ward up on BYU campus. I was called to lead the BYU 55th Ward and during the initial first weeks I was going through the ward records and saw where Brother Ed was Bishop of the same BYU 55th Ward back in the late 1970's. I went home and called Brother Pinegar, who at that time was serving in a Stake Presidency in Orem and when I told him of the coincidence he let out a big laugh. I then asked him if he would come and do a fireside for the young people in our ward. He hesitated for a moment and then said, "Normally I don't do that anymore up on campus, but for you the answer is of course . . . 'Yes'." The next Sunday night he came and delivered a wonderful message to the 150 members of my ward and the students loved him(. . . .) Many of you have your favorite Ed Pinegar story . . . he blessed and enriched the lives of thousands of people with his teaching and his love for his fellowman.—"Let your light so shine before men, that they may see your good works, and glorify your Father which is in heaven."

If you had the privilege of knowing Brother Ed, you probably heard him say in that unmistakable, raspy voice of his, "I love you. I love you. I love you!" And you believed him. Those who knew him felt his love because Brother Ed always shared *His* love, the love of the Savior, wherever he went. Brother Ed generously shared PIE with the world, and we were better for it.

Much love,

Kristin McQuivey
Editor and Coauthor

Acknowledgments

IT IS WITH GRATITUDE AND love that I express my thanks to all the missionaries of the England London South Mission who lived the principles of expressing love to others through praise, inspiration, and encouragement. Special thanks to my assistants and sister leaders who were giving love to all the missionaries as they worked with them. I am honored and grateful for Elders David Hirschi and David Covey, who wrote the foreword.

Special thanks to my longtime friend and coauthor of many books, Richard J. Allen, who gave inspired input and provided great editorial help to the manuscript. He was a lifesaver. Special thanks to my great editors Kathy Jenkins Oveson and Kristin McQuivey. To my many friends who have helped me along the way, I am forever grateful.

I am continually amazed at the presence and power of the Holy Ghost, who inspired and led me to see the power praise, inspiration, and encouragement can have as we express love one to another. I express gratitude to my Savior Jesus Christ and my Heavenly Father for the two great commandments concerning love.

And as always, I am thankful to my sweetheart, Pat, who is very patient with me as I sit hunched over my computer with my three little fingers typing.

Foreword

THIS FOREWORD WAS WRITTEN BY David M. Hirschi and David M. R. Covey, who served with Brother Pinegar while he was the mission president in the England London South Mission. Brother Pinegar said of his time working with them: "Elder Hirschi and Elder Covey, along with Sister Pedersen and Sister Perkins, were simply magnificent trainers. They truly loved the missionaries and were the ones who helped everyone have a great and perfect day on their mission. All the missionaries loved them for who they were— true disciples, meek and humble servants of the Lord."

It is our honor to write the foreword of this book on behalf of our beloved mission president, Ed Jolley Pinegar. When President Pinegar arrived in the England London South Mission (ELSM), which covered the southeast corner of England, in July of 1985, the mission and the missionaries were completely unaware of how dramatically their lives were about to change—for the better.

President Pinegar exuded love, inspiration, and enthusiasm in every fiber of his being. One day, he called us in for a three-hour meeting prior to doing "workovers" with all the companionships. We went over every aspect of what it would take for a missionary to have a great day in serving the Lord. He called it having a "perfect" day. Nothing was overlooked in the effort to be exactly and immediately obedient. Then he discussed how we were to represent the Lord in this precious assignment.

We were to be meek and lowly and serve the missionaries with humility and love. We needed to look for the good and compliment them often. In companionship study, we were to inspire them to new heights as we used the scriptures and help them see the power of the Holy Ghost, who would assist them as they faithfully served. We were to appropriately encourage them in every way possible so they would know they could do the work. We were to cheer them on after each finding and teaching moment throughout the day. As we carried out our assignment, expressing love throughout the day had a great effect on us as assistants—and the missionaries were smiling and happy while doing the work. It was amazing.

Serving as missionaries in the ELSM was no picnic. In fact, it was downright difficult, challenging, and sometimes even depressing. The people who lived in our mission were quiet and reserved. They liked to keep to themselves. In fact, one of the most common statements people made when contacted by the missionaries was "I keep meself to meself, lad, and do no one no harm." It wasn't exactly a formula for a successful dialogue.

It was extremely difficult to really talk with people, let alone connect with them about their religious beliefs or share a religious message. I remember a man saying to us on the first week of my mission, "The English people don't like discussing religion or talking to religious people. Stick to the weather, lads, and you'll do just fine here."

Wow. We were in for a long two years.

That was before President Pinegar.

President Pinegar modeled the pattern of expressing love as he visited with us. He always had a good word for all the missionaries, and he inspired us to carry on. When he arrived in the mission, the ELSM was baptizing an average of twenty-five to thirty-five people per month, with a recent yearly high of fifty. He said we would be baptizing more than one hundred people per month within one year's time.

Feeling a bit skeptical, we wondered how on earth *that* was going to happen.

Well, President Pinegar knew *exactly* how it was going to happen.

He began by recognizing and praising our strengths as well as our efforts. Next, he helped to inspire us by increasing our vision and our productivity individually and collectively as a mission. He did this by constantly teaching us true and proven missionary principles and doctrines and by giving us constant praise and recognition for our efforts and accomplishments.

True to his vision, one year later—down to the month—it happened: We baptized 115 people in July 1986.

As an instrument in the Lord's hands, President Pinegar helped change our missions—and later, our lives—with simple but powerful expressions of love. As assistants, we had quietly called President Pinegar's mandate of expressing love with praise, inspiration, and encouragement "PIE." "Give them PIE" became our little acronym to express love with genuine praise, inspiration by the power of the Holy Ghost, and continual encouragement along the way.

Let us illustrate how President Pinegar exemplified each of these three characteristics so impeccably:

PRAISE

President Pinegar knew how to give specific praise. This is far different from general praise. When a person praises a specific characteristic or attribute, he or she really cares about you and knows you. That was the kind of praise President Pinegar knew how to give. Whether the praise was face-to-face or in a letter, he was masterful in his delivery.

This specific praise made us and the missionaries in the ELSM willing to walk through walls for President Pinegar. We each wanted to be the person he envisioned we could be, even though we all felt inadequate. But we became laser-focused with becoming the best we could be, and above all, we did not want to disappoint him. President Pinegar's praise made good missionaries into great missionaries.

INSPIRATION

President Pinegar invoked missionary stories from the Book of Mormon (his favorite book) to inspire his missionaries. No missionary from the ELSM can ever read Alma 29:9 (Alma being an instrument in the hands of God), Alma 26 (Ammon rejoicing in mission success), Mosiah 28:3 (the desire of the sons of Mosiah to save souls), or Alma 17:2–3 (describing the preparation required of the Lord's missionaries) without hearing and feeling President Pinegar's voice. He made these scriptures come alive. And he inspired all of his missionaries with the vision that they, too, could become like these missionaries of old.

ENCOURAGEMENT

Finally, President Pinegar provided the encouragement all missionaries needed to succeed. The word *encourage* means to "give support, confidence, or hope" to someone. Being a missionary and doing missionary work requires great courage. Courage to step outside of yourself. Courage to face people who will mock and ridicule you. Courage to believe that better times are ahead. Courage to believe that there is a family waiting to hear your message. And courage to press on when things look bleak. President Pinegar provided this support, this confidence, and this hope to all his missionaries.

The belief that we could become powerful missionaries was deeply ingrained and entrenched in ELSM missionaries because of the praise, inspiration, and encouragement provided by President Pinegar and our other mission leaders. We were unleashed, ready and prepared to become mighty instruments in the hands of God to perform HIS work. And as the Prophet Joseph Smith said, "After all that has been said, the greatest and most important duty is to preach the Gospel."[1]

We believed it, and we lived it. But President Pinegar enabled it.

David M. Hirschi
David M. R. Covey

---

1   *Teachings of the Prophet Joseph Smith*, comp. Joseph Fielding Smith (Salt Lake City: Deseret Book, 1938), 113.

Introduction

THIS BOOK IS DESIGNED FOR you—parents, teachers, and leaders—to help you make an impact and difference in the lives of those you love, teach, lead, and associate with. The words on these pages will teach you principles that will help you create an atmosphere for learning and assist others in achieving their goals and aspirations in life. You will come to understand and appreciate the power of love and ways it can be expressed that will make a difference in the lives of those you seek to serve and bless.

This short book had its beginning thirty-five years ago in London, England, while I was serving as president of the England London South Mission (1985–1988). I was prompted to have my two assistants, David Hirschi and David Covey, do exchanges with all the elders and have a "perfect day" with them proselyting. I didn't want it to be just a "training day," but a *perfect day* as a missionary. Training sisters Sharlene Pederson and Rebecca Perkins would do the same thing with the sister missionaries.

I met with Elder Hirschi and Elder Covey for two or three hours and discussed all the aspects that would lead one to have a great day, a successful day, a joy-filled day on their mission. It was to be a day that reflected exact and joyful obedience, one in which they were prompted and led by the Holy Spirit. It was also to be a day that the missionaries could duplicate after the assistants were gone.

This "perfect day" included every aspect of a missionary's day—arising early in the morning, exercising, doing companionship study, and putting in a full day of missionary work. In the process, they were counseled to pray fervently and with faith to teach and love the missionaries and to build a good relationship of trust by being meek and humble and serving them in every possible way. They were to be the missionaries' Christlike servants and leaders. They were to see the good in the missionaries and compliment them on their efforts and the things they were doing well. Their instruction to the missionaries was to be inspired by the Holy Spirit and was to help them do better, be better, and find joy in the work.

As each of the exchanges began, the assistants and trainers pled with the Lord for an outpouring of the Holy Spirit as they worked and traveled. Throughout the day and again at the end of the day, they gave the missionaries they were working with the encouragement to carry on. They were expressing love to the missionaries, and the missionaries were motivated.

The results of these "perfect days" were amazing. Missionaries wrote me letters that were filled with detailed commentary of their day's activities. They had success, they were happy in the work, and they enjoyed the experience. They were enthusiastic and loved doing the work of the

Lord by inviting people to come unto Christ. They routinely mentioned how good they felt doing the Lord's work.

They saw their leaders in a whole new light, describing how much they loved the assistants and the sister leaders. They spoke of the inspired teaching they had observed and the compliments they had received in letters and phone calls. Their days were better and more successful, and the work was progressing. With enthusiasm, they declared, "I can have a great day every day on my mission."

In answering the missionaries' letters, I also expressed my love. Over the next year or so of expressing love through praise, inspiration, and encouragement, the missionaries and I gave that process the quiet title of PIE. PIE (Praise, Inspiration, Encouragement) is an expression of love. It is *not* something we do to people. It is not a technique. It is heartfelt sharing of Christlike love for others. As we shared PIE in the mission, lives were changed, and everyone was happy in the work.

The effect of PIE didn't stop with the missionaries who paired up with the leaders. On the weekends, I received reports from the assistants and the sister leaders. Over time, we all gained a great testimony of leading those we serve with love and helping them achieve their expectations as disciples of the Lord. They were indeed the Lord's disciples: "A new commandment I give unto you, That ye love one another; as I have loved you, that ye also love one another. By this shall all men know that ye are my disciples, if ye have love one to another."[1] Indeed, the missionary leaders were "loving one another" and assisting the missionaries in feeding the Lord's sheep and bringing souls to Christ.[2]

---

1   John 13:34–35.
2   See John 21:15–17; D&C 15:6; 18:10–16.

Over time, the missionaries came to know that they were valuable instruments in the hands of the Lord and that they had great potential. They realized they could do many things of their own free will. They could achieve their goals. They could make a difference in another person's life.

To be loved is the greatest need of the human soul. God the Father[3] and our Savior Jesus Christ[4] are the perfect examples of doing all that They do in love—because They love us.

There is nothing that can give one a greater sense of accomplishment than helping others. The greatest joy is loving and serving others so that they might come unto Christ and enjoy the blessings of exaltation. And there is nothing that can give one a greater feeling of worth and a greater measure of joy in life than strengthening and serving others.[5]

How can you begin your quest to praise, inspire, and encourage others to be their best? *Look for opportunities to praise, inspire, and encourage others!* If you are willing to reach out and test the principles and concepts contained in this little book, there is a great reward awaiting you. The read is short. The underlying principles are sound and easily learned and practiced. All that is required is a desire to express love in many ways—a desire to care for and help others a little more each day. With that desire, you will become more aware each day of the treasure trove of opportunities for service that abound on every side, around every corner, and in every shadow. With that desire, you will discover the courage to

---

3   See John 3:16.

4   See 2 Nephi 26:24.

5   See D&C 81:5; 108:7.

act, frequently going out of your way—even beyond your comfort zone—to become involved with others and bless their lives. This can become the transcending experience of your life. You literally become regenerated in life as you see the good in others and help them achieve success in every facet of their lives.

You have the power to bless and lead others to be better and do better when you have *a true, Christlike desire to love others!*

That is how you begin your quest to bless and serve others: by giving everyone a morsel of goodness and serving them with love through PIE. If you can just learn to give everyone a piece of PIE as often as possible, you will unfold for yourself and for others the abundance of life and the riches of happiness and joy. This isn't just applicable in the mission field when dealing with discouraged missionaries. This is applicable everywhere! Anywhere you want to be an influence for good and inspire those around you to be happier and more effective, serve up some PIE!

But remember, PIE isn't something you do to people. You love people and express that love in many ways. You will find that expressing love in this way will be fulfilling and longer lasting as you seek to bless and serve others.

Chapter 1
WHAT IS PIE?

PRAISE, INSPIRATION, AND ENCOURAGEMENT

STOP! TAKE A MOMENT TO reread and ponder the introduction. Can you think of an area in your life that would benefit from some PIE?

First, let's discover a little bit more about what PIE is.

PIE is an acronym for expressing love to others. We're not talking about pie you make with pumpkin and canned milk (although I love that kind of pie too). The ingredients we're looking for are praise, inspiration, and encouragement—hence the simple acronym P–I–E.

Here's exactly what we mean by PIE:

PRAISE

Praise is a form of complimenting and congratulating another for his or her efforts, which can revitalize the soul. Honest and genuine praise lifts, motivates, provides a sense of approval, and gives honor to and acceptance of a person's worth and performance. All these things enhance a person's well-being.

Praise dispels doubt and fear and builds confidence. Praise gives hope—the power to move forward without discouragement or despair. Hope energizes us to carry on. Praise received from a respected source opens the vista to achieving the unimaginable. Praise strengthens the relationship and opens the hearts of others to your welcome expression of love.

It is not only to those around us that we express love through praise. We express our love and gratitude to our Father in Heaven through praise as well, as is shown repeatedly in the scriptures. Look at how many times we are told to praise God in the book of Psalms alone! When you honestly praise God and He sees you as a yearning child reaching out to Him, He knows of your love for Him and your desire to please Him.

As you praise God and others, your mind will focus on holier matters—loving God and your fellow men. Praising others always increases your level of meekness and humility. Praising others lifts both the giver and the receiver, because honest praise is a form and expression of the pure love of Christ. Elder Neal A. Maxwell wrote, "We should, therefore, without being artificial, regularly give deserved, specific praise."[1]

INSPIRATION

Inspiration is anchored in the blessings and power of the Holy Ghost. The Holy Ghost will teach you what to say and do as you teach those you serve.[2] Through the power of the Holy Ghost, you help them come to the knowledge of the Lord and truth.[3]

---

1   Neal A. Maxwell, *All These Things Shall Give Thee Experience* (Salt Lake City: Deseret Book, 2009), 78.

2   See 2 Nephi 32:5; D&C 68:3–7; 100:4–5.

3   See Alma 23:5–6.

As you teach others eternal truths from the word of God, their understanding and appreciation will be increased, and they will be filled with gratitude. Gratitude is the catalyst for change. You can change your attitude and your behavior for the better when you are grateful for something or someone. Moroni taught:

> Behold, I would exhort you that when ye shall read these things, if it be wisdom in God that ye should read them, that ye would remember how merciful the Lord hath been unto the children of men, from the creation of Adam even down until the time that ye shall receive these things, and ponder it in your hearts.[4]

When eternal truths are given through the power of the Holy Ghost, they are given with persuasion, gentleness, patience, kindness, clarity, and charity. Inspiration and motivation to do better will flourish in a relationship of trust—one where credibility has been established and the person is eager to change and move forward in life. It's a matter of synergy, with the teacher and the learner working together in harmony by the Spirit of Truth.[5]

When you seek to bless others to do good, you become a conduit for the Holy Spirit to inspire and lift one of God's children. When you are an instrument in the hand of God, you become a disciple of one of Christ's greatest desires—the desire to lift, inspire, enthuse, console, and help another be all

4   Moroni 10:3.

5   See D&C 50:17–25.

they can be. Indeed, Christ called the commandment to "love thy neighbour as thyself" one of the greatest commandments we've been given—second only to loving God Himself.[6]

Blessing another soul in any way is part of ministering and is part of the gathering of Israel. This is one of the greatest things you can do as a servant of God.[7] Every act that strengthens another to do good is a result of the empowerment of the Holy Spirit[8] and the grace of God.

ENCOURAGEMENT

Encouragement is the sunshine that generates growth. It should be natural and spontaneous, regular and frequent, gentle and polite—never overbearing or crude. Provide encouragement for a specific purpose: so people will have the strength and courage to go on faithfully, to continue steadfastly, and to be resilient.

When moments of challenge enter our lives—and they will come—we often look to our leaders, support groups, or close friends for encouragement. Those receiving encouragement from their parents, teachers, and leaders will have a safety net to help them change, improve, and achieve their goals. You can be that kind of protector as you encourage others along the covenant path. Giving encouragement to people you love is an act that has eternal impact—your life-changing act will ripple through their lives to people unknown to you.

Seeking to encourage others will open a new vista in your life. Each day, a ray of sunshine will radiate from your lips and shower someone with hope, confidence, courage, and

---

6   See Matthew 22:36–40.

7   See Alma 29:9–10; D&C 15:6.

8   See D&C 11:12–13.

optimism to carry on with renewed vigor and vitality. Don't doubt the power of encouragement, for it is the untapped source of inner strength.

Praise, inspiration, and encouragement are linked together and are integrally connected. Because of this, they are often expressed together. Amulek explains this principle:

> And as ye have desired of my beloved brother that he should make known unto you what ye should do, because of your afflictions; and he hath spoken somewhat unto you to prepare your minds (inspired instruction); yea, and he hath exhorted (encouraged) you unto faith and to patience.[9]

Inspired instruction followed by exhortation is the strongest form of encouragement. In his last address, Moroni encouraged us with every fiber of his being. As part of that, he used a form of the word *exhort* nine times in Moroni 10. To put that in its proper context, note that this form of the word *exhort* is used only twenty times in the entire Book of Mormon.

It's important to understand what exactly an exhortation is and its place in giving PIE. An exhortation is defined as "an address or communication emphatically urging someone to do something"[10] or "language intended to incite and

---

9   Alma 34:3.
10   "Exhortation," *Lexico.com*, 2020, https://www.lexico.com/en/definition/exhortation (November 2020).

encourage."[11] Oftentimes, we may read an exhortation in the scriptures as a command or form of instruction, but at its core, it is truly a form of encouragement—a call to do better, to be better. In a way, an exhortation is much like a pep talk from an encouraging coach who tells us, "Let's go out there, give it our all, and win!"

Consider this exhortation from Moroni as an example:

> Behold, I would exhort you that when ye shall read these things, if it be wisdom in God that ye should read them, that ye would remember how merciful the Lord hath been unto the children of men, from the creation of Adam even down until the time that ye shall receive these things, and ponder it in your hearts.[12]

While this may sound like instruction, consider the things that Moroni is asking us to do—to read, to remember, and to ponder. These words are not a strict commandment or instruction manual; they are "intended to incite and encourage,"[13] to drive us to become closer to our Father in Heaven through study and prayer. They are an exhortation and an encouragement to strive for our potential. We, too, can use exhortations when giving PIE to others by reminding them of their own celestial potential and encouraging them to reach it.

---

11   "Exhortation," *Merriam-Webster.com*, 2020, https://www.merriam-webster.com/dictionary/exhortation (November 2020).

12   Moroni 10:3.

13   "Exhortation," *Merriam-Webster.com*.

When you give others PIE, you go about doing *good* like the Savior did when He was anointed by God the Father: "How God anointed Jesus of Nazareth with the Holy Ghost and with power: who went about doing good, and healing all that were oppressed of the devil; for God was with him."[14] It is the power and grace of God through which our Savior went about doing good, "for every thing which inviteth to do good, and to persuade to believe in Christ, is sent forth by the power and gift of Christ; wherefore ye may know with a perfect knowledge it is of God."[15]

Remember, it is through the grace of God that you can do good. "For we are his workmanship, created in Christ Jesus unto good works, which God hath before ordained that we should walk in them."[16] The Holy Ghost is such a great gift from God the Father because the Holy Spirit "leadeth to do good."[17]

PIE relies on faith, hope, and charity—three qualities that are integrally connected as they work synergistically to help us do good. "And see that ye have faith, hope, and charity, and then ye will always abound in good works."[18]

When PIE is part of the equation, *everyone* wins—the one who gives and the one who receives. The bottom line is this: you can get rich by loving others—rich with charity and love, with many blessings measured in increased self-confidence, self-worth and self-esteem, self-respect, resilience, thankfulness, and lasting joy.

14   Acts 10:38.

15   Moroni 7:16; see also verses 12–15.

16   Ephesians 2:10.

17   D&C 11:12.

18   Alma 7:24.

PIE IS AN EXPRESSION OF CHARITY

PIE is simply one of the many ways to express charity, the pure love of Christ. The blessing of charity will help you praise, inspire, and encourage. You love others when you possess the pure love of Christ that God the Father bestows upon the true followers of His Son.[19]

What is this charity, this pure love of Christ, you feel? Charity is generous, patient, slow to provocation, has no envy, is kind, and, above all, is benevolent toward others. It has concern for those in need—which includes all men, for aren't we all in need of love and acceptance? It is forbearing; it is not persuaded to judge harshly but rather to be tolerant of others' needs, concerns, and situations. Charity is tender, compassionate, caring, thoughtful, and gracious.

Because it shows concern and compassion for others, PIE is a demonstration of the pure love of Christ. The pure love of Christ is multifaceted, illustrating purpose and power. Everything through time and all eternity hinges on love. If you don't have the love of God, you become subject to contention, envying, strife, and all kinds of tumults. But every problem, affliction, trial, and adversity can be healed by the Lord's Atonement and the grace of God—the two greatest expressions of God's love. You need the love of God in your heart to be willing to help people.

Every expression of Christ is a form of love, which is why charity is described as "the pure love of Christ."[20] It is constant and enduring, and when you possess charity, you are rewarded with Mormon's promise, "that when (Christ) shall appear we shall be like him, for we shall see him as he is."[21]

19   See Moroni 7:48.

20   Moroni 7:47.

21   Moroni 7:48.

As you come to understand charity, you will realize that it is a gift you can receive from God the Father as you become a true follower of His Son, Jesus Christ.[22] This is where you can begin preparing to give PIE—by becoming more charitable yourself. Read and ponder Mormon's inspiring words in Moroni 7:44–48. Remember that the pure love of Christ "suffereth long, and is kind, and envieth not, and is not puffed up, seeketh not her own, is not easily provoked, thinketh no evil, and rejoiceth not in iniquity but rejoiceth in the truth, beareth all things, believeth all things, hopeth all things, endureth all things."[23]

Can you really become a charitable person with the pure love of Christ in your heart? YES! As you follow Christ, you become like unto Christ, and He will perfect you.

> Yea, come unto Christ, and be perfected in him, and deny yourselves of all ungodliness; and if ye shall deny yourselves of all ungodliness, and love God with all your might, mind and strength, then is his grace sufficient for you, that by his grace ye may be perfect in Christ; and if by the grace of God ye are perfect in Christ, ye can in nowise deny the power of God.
>
> And again, if ye by the grace of God are perfect in Christ, and deny not his power, then are ye sanctified in Christ by the grace of God, through the shedding of the blood of Christ, which is in the covenant of the

---

22 See Moroni 7:48.
23 Moroni 7:45.

> Father unto the remission of your sins, that
> ye become holy, without spot.[24]

That might sound daunting; in fact, some might think it is asking too much. Remember, in the strength of the Lord, you can do all things. As Nephi stated in 1 Nephi 3:7, "The Lord giveth no commandments unto the children of men, save he shall prepare a way for them that they may accomplish the thing which he commandeth them." We see further testament of this in Alma 26:11–12, when Ammon professes that "in (God's) strength I can do all things."[25]

Yes, you can be strengthened in the Lord to do all things requested of you, as the scriptures promise. And He has asked you to love God and one another.[26]

You see, the only way you can give PIE is to have love and an "abundance mentality"—the belief that there is plenty of everything: opportunities, love, friends, and chances to succeed in life. We are not competing for or hoarding these limited resources; there is enough for all.

You must begin to think of others instead of yourself. Selfishness often destroys relationships in marriages, in families, and in the workplace. So that is where you begin making the change—by starting to think of others and thus initiating the process of becoming a loving person. This is a process, not an event, and you begin by doing it one step at a time. The promised blessings are immediate: you start to feel better right away.

---

24   Moroni 10:32–33.

25   See also Philippians 4:13.

26   See Matthew 22:36–40.

As you take each step toward charity and giving PIE to others, the truthfulness of what you are doing will be reinforced. "If any man will do his will, he shall know of the doctrine, whether it be of God, or whether I speak of myself. He that speaketh of himself seeketh his own glory: but he that seeketh his glory that sent him, the same is true, and no unrighteousness is in him."[27] You will prove this eternal truth empirically as you live it. You will find joy and happiness in the things you do—blessing others. Charity and the power of the Holy Ghost work together in expressing love.

Why are some people able to compliment and praise others so naturally and graciously? Because they are loving and confident with themselves—they know who they are and what they can do. They are people with an abundance mentality. They are full of charity and love. They sense that there is an unlimited supply of love, compliments, and praise—more than enough to go around. They find joy in lifting others and giving others the credit where credit is due, and they seek not to toot their own horn but rather stand back and give the accolades to others. This is what charity can do for you— you see the good in others, just waiting to be discovered. You find joy in seeing others' eyes light up with gratitude and thanksgiving for being appreciated or complimented for who they are or for what they have done.

PIE is what you express to everybody—coworkers, team members, family, friends, students, teachers, leaders, and even strangers. You see, everyone needs love, and PIE is a way to express that in a very positive way.

---

27   John 7:17–18.

We all need PIE from each other. We all need to strengthen and bless one another—this is part of the second great commandment, "Thou shalt love thy neighbour as thyself."[28] Because everyone needs PIE, you need to be a giver of PIE, but you need to give it in a natural and genuine way with real intent. It cannot be a canned presentation. It cannot be a form of manipulation. You don't force-feed anyone PIE. You never give someone course after course of PIE. As you give PIE, remember that it is best received in smaller doses; that's the philosophy behind random acts of kindness—they are usually small gestures that are spontaneously given.

A NOTE ON RECEIVING PIE

While the focus of this book is on how to give PIE, it's also important that you are able to recognize when PIE is being served to you—and to receive it graciously and gratefully. Of course, knowing how to give PIE will also make it easier to recognize when it's being given to you. So how do you receive PIE from others? With a genuine thank-you and a sincere expression of "You are so kind." You should not feel the need to reject PIE when it's given. You are being uplifted with genuine love! Receive it with a smile!

EXPRESSING LOVE BY THE POWER OF THE HOLY GHOST

The Holy Ghost will show you all things to do and will prompt you to praise, inspire, and encourage. "Again I say unto you that if ye will enter in by the way, and receive the Holy Ghost, it will show unto you all things what ye should do."[29] When you trust in the Holy Spirit, you will go about

28 Matthew 22:39.
29 2 Nephi 32:5.

doing good: "And now, verily, verily, I say unto thee, put your trust in that Spirit which leadeth to do good."[30] And that goodness is followed by many blessings of the Spirit: "to do justly, to walk humbly, to judge righteously; and this is my Spirit. Verily, verily, I say unto you, I will impart unto you of my Spirit, which shall enlighten your mind, which shall fill your soul with joy."[31]

The pure love of Christ—charity—works in concert with the Holy Ghost to do good and to be motivated by love. Love is one of the many precious fruits of the Spirit: "But the fruit of the Spirit is love, joy, peace, longsuffering, gentleness, goodness, faith, meekness, temperance: against such there is no law."[32]

Expressing love through praising others, inspiring them to do better and be better, and continually encouraging them will bring great blessings to both giver and receiver. Over time, the love within your heart and the presence and power of the Holy Spirit will take root in your soul, and you will express love through PIE naturally because that is who you are. To become that kind of person, you must not only be a true follower of our Savior Jesus Christ, but you must be worthy of the companionship and power of the Holy Ghost.

PREPARING TO BE WORTHY OF THE HOLY GHOST

Receiving the gift of the Holy Ghost by priesthood authority is far from the end of the story. If you want to have the constant companionship of the Holy Ghost, you must be worthy of that companionship. As your spirituality increases,

30 D&C 11:12.
31 D&C 11:12–13.
32 Galatians 5:22–23.

the fruits of the presence of the Holy Ghost will increase in your life. The nine scriptures that follow provide a blueprint on how to gain the companionship of the Holy Ghost:

1. **Be meek and lowly.** Through the remission of sins, you become meek and lowly and are worthy of "*the visitation of the Holy Ghost.*"[33]

2. **Increase your faith in the Lord Jesus Christ.** Lehi "spake by the power of the Holy Ghost, *which power he received by faith on the Son of God.*"[34]

3. **Feast upon the Word of God by the power of the Holy Ghost.** The Lord reminds us, "Angels speak by the power of the Holy Ghost; wherefore, they speak the words of Christ. Wherefore, I said unto you, *feast upon the words of Christ; for behold, the words of Christ will tell you all things what ye should do.*"[35] The Holy Ghost will also "*show unto you all things what ye should do.*"[36]

4. **Always remember our Savior Jesus Christ.** "And *always remember him* . . . that they may always have his Spirit to be with them. Amen."[37]

5. **Be obedient and seek righteousness.** "*Keep his commandments which he has given* (you); that (you) may always have his Spirit to be with (you)."[38]

6. **Love God with all your heart, might, mind, and strength.** Remember that the things of God "are only to

---

33   Moroni 8:26; emphasis added.

34   1 Nephi 10:17; emphasis added.

35   2 Nephi 32:3; emphasis added.

36   2 Nephi 32:5; emphasis added.

37   D&C 20:77; emphasis added.

38   D&C 20:77; emphasis added.

be seen and understood by the power of the Holy Spirit, *which God bestows on those who love him.*"[39]

7. **Purify yourself through righteousness and the grace of God.** As emphasized in the previous segment, the works of the Lord and the mysteries of the kingdom "are only to be seen and understood by the power of the Holy Spirit, which God bestows on those who love him, and *purify themselves before him.*"[40]

8. **Be endowed with power from on high so that you can receive a fullness of the Holy Ghost.** "And that they may grow up in thee, and *receive a fulness of the Holy Ghost,* and be organized according to thy laws, and be prepared to obtain every needful thing."[41] Alma Burton, former president of the Manti Temple, wrote in the *Encyclopedia of Mormonism,* "Through the temple endowment, one may seek 'a fulness of the Holy Ghost' (D&C 109:15). Temple ordinances are seen as a means for receiving inspiration and instruction through the Holy Spirit, and for preparing to return to the presence of God."[42]

9. **Plead in your prayers to be filled with the Holy Spirit.**[43] And plead to have the Spirit poured out upon the people you seek to help.[44]

When you understand and implement the things you need to do, as described above, you will have the blessing

---

39 D&C 76:116; emphasis added.
40 D&C 76:116; emphasis added.
41 D&C 109:15; emphasis added.
42 Alma P. Burton, "Endowment," *Encyclopedia of Mormonism,* ed. Daniel H. Ludlow, vol. 1 (New York: Macmillan, 1992), 455.
43 See Alma 18:16; Helaman 5:45.
44 See Mosiah 4:20; Alma 8:10; 19:14.

of the Holy Ghost in your life. You will begin to recognize His presence and power in your life as you become attuned to His promptings and manifestations.

His presence is the priceless and unspeakable gift for all of us in mortality. It is the gift from God that will help you love and serve your brothers and sisters. Expressing love to others is the joy of being a disciple of Christ.[45] With the presence of the Holy Ghost, you are directed by the Spirit in your life, and you are shown all things that you should do and say and be.[46] (To learn more about the blessings of the Holy Ghost, see chapters 3 and 6.)

REMEMBER—EVERYONE NEEDS LOVE AND ACCEPTANCE

The overwhelming desire of the human soul is to be loved and accepted. If a person wants to function well and feel good about himself or herself, emotional needs must be met, including the need to be loved and accepted.

I once had the opportunity to give a presentation to a large audience, and I wanted to demonstrate the power of receiving a verbal expression of love. I asked everyone in the audience to turn to the people seated around them and tell each of them, "I love you." Within minutes, everyone was talking and laughing with each other. Faces were smiling. People were animated. Some even gave an unsuspecting person a hug. All of that followed such a simple thing. Three little words—I love you—resulted in so much goodness. It took me a while to get everyone's attention back from this enjoyable experience, and when I did, they were all smiling and feeling good.

---

45   See John 13:34–35; 21:15–17.
46   See 2 Nephi 32:5; D&C 11:12–13; 68:3–7.

Everyone needs to be told that they are loved. Everyone needs to give love. Oh, there are cynics who say, "You just don't do that." And that is their problem. Love is a commandment, yet we guard it like it is a commodity we can never replace if we spend it—when the opposite is true. The more love you give, the more love you have. The more love you give, the better you feel. Whenever you are down and are feeling depressed and sorry for yourself, go bless someone. Go serve someone with praise, inspiration, and encouragement, and simply express love with those three little words: *I love you*. Yes, you will feel better. It works. Try it!

Love can be expressed in a variety of ways. You can say, "I love you." You can pull on your earlobe, wink your eye, give a hug, stand and look with approval at someone special—the list goes on. In every case, the essential ingredient is that you are expressing affection and approval to someone.

Just remember that demonstrating love takes time. You've heard people say, "My dad took me to the ball game." "My mom took me shopping and out to lunch." "My teacher encouraged me to succeed all by myself." "Bill stayed after work and helped me finish my project." All those expressions are demonstrations of love—and they took time. Time is so precious and can never be stored up or recovered. You use it wisely by lifting and serving others.

People who are loved and accepted feel a sense of self-worth. Their self-esteem and self-respect are bolstered, and they are renewed in their efforts to succeed. That's not a false sense of esteem. True self-esteem comes from within—from knowing we are the divine children of God the Father. Without that conviction, we can believe that our self-esteem and self-worth are tied to things like possessions, positions, titles, or stations. Those "things" are not the standard by which we gauge ourselves or others. We must never forget that we are all individuals of worth. When we recognize who we are—our divine nature—and what we can become, we will change for the better. That is the power of love and PIE.

Remember, love is the motive for everything God the Father does: "For God so loved the world, that he gave his only begotten Son, that whosoever believeth in him should not perish, but have everlasting life."[47] Love is the motive for everything our Savior Jesus Christ does: "He (our Savior Jesus Christ) doeth not anything save it be for the benefit of the world; for he loveth the world, even that he layeth down his own life that he may draw all men unto him. Wherefore, he commandeth none that they shall not partake of his salvation."[48] Their love is constant and complete, for They seek our immortality and eternal life.[49]

AN EXPERIMENT WITH ETERNAL REWARDS

I had a glorious experience with promptings of the Holy Ghost as I was teaching a lesson to my seminary class in 1966. We were covering the subject of love and expressing love. The students all seemed to be anxiously engaged in the conversation of the day. I got the idea (a prompting from the Holy Ghost) to ask for a volunteer to do a special homework assignment. Following that prompting, I stopped the conversation and asked, "Who will do me a favor?"

---

47   John 3:16.
48   2 Nephi 26:24.
49   See Moses 1:39.

The hands flew up. Dennis Dunn, a young boy near the back of the room, seemed especially eager. I called him up to the front and asked, "Dennis, do you really want to do this favor for me?"

"Sure!"

"This is really hard," I warned him.

"I can do it. That's no problem. I can do it," he said.

"Well, this is really going to take some effort," I said.

In exasperation, he said, "I'll do it. Just what do you want me to do?"

"When you go home tonight, call out for your mother. When your mother comes to you, take her in your arms and give her a big embrace. Then give her a big kiss. And then whisper in her ear, 'Oh, Mommy, I love you.'"

Dennis stopped, looked at me, and said, "No way! No way can I do that."

"Dennis, do you love your mother?"

"Of course I do."

"Then why can't you do it?"

"You just don't do things like that," he replied.

"Dennis, if you love her, you should tell her."

"No way!" he said.

Dennis and I were pretty good friends, so I said to him, "Dennis, I think I can hear a chicken clucking in this class." The class all started to laugh, and I could tell Dennis felt uneasy. "In fact, Dennis, I think there's a yellow stripe coming right up your back." Now everyone in the class was laughing—even Dennis. In fact, he was laughing the loudest. It was all done in the spirit of fun.

After we played around for a minute, Dennis finally relented and said, "Okay, okay, I'll do it." *The Holy Spirit won.*

Dennis went back to his seat, the class period ended, and life went on.

The next day as I was greeting the members of the class, I saw Dennis and asked, "Dennis, how did it go last night?"

He looked at me and said, "Oh, it was wonderful!" (Clearly, Dennis had experienced the fruits and power of the Holy Spirit.)

"Can you tell me about it?"

"Can I tell the whole class?" he asked.

"You're on," I said. After the class devotional, I said, "We have a special report today from Dennis."

Dennis came up to the front. As he stood in front of the class, he was still the big junior in high school, but something was different. His lips began to quiver, and his eyes began to fill up with tears. Then he blurted out, "Oh, you guys, it was the greatest day of my life. It seemed like my mom cried for hours. I can't believe it." They all laughed.

Then he said, clearly following the prompting of the Holy Spirit, "You don't realize what we've done to our parents. We've locked them out of our lives. They've done everything for us, and we treat them like dirt. We should be ashamed. They're starved for our love just like we're starved for their love. But you've gotta say it. You've gotta tell 'em." The class was on fire. But Dennis didn't leave it there. He continued, "You've all gotta go home and do it just like I did."

At that moment, silent commitments were made by the kids in that class, and they went home and did it—just like Dennis described. The Holy Spirit prompted them to act.

A couple of weeks went by, and we had a night where parents came and visited with the teachers. I had all the parents sit in the chairs where their children sat during class. I stood up in front and told them that our class was discussing the New Testament and the teachings of our Savior. One parent asked, "What do you do in this class?"

I attempted to explain again.

"No, you don't understand," she said. "My son's nice to me now. He even told me he loved me. And the only thing I can think of that's been different in his life lately is this class."

Other hands shot into the air; other parents said the same thing had happened to them. Now the parents were on fire. Suddenly these parents felt so good about their children. What they were really feeling was the comfort and peace of the Holy Ghost. When I responded, I merely said, "Oh, it's just their goodness. You've just learned how good your children really are."

Lives were changed by Dennis Dunn's experience. He made a difference in all the lives of those young people, for he set an example and challenged them by the power of the Holy Ghost. They took the challenge and made the commitment, and families were blessed. With the power of the Holy Ghost, they all expressed their love. Parents were happy, families were happy, and life was beautiful.

THE KEY TO EXPRESSING LOVE: THE POWER OF THE HOLY SPIRIT AND THE PURE LOVE OF CHRIST WORKING TOGETHER

As a mission president, I learned that revelation (inspiration) is essential in all things because the Holy Spirit directs our lives for good, just as it did Dennis Dunn's life. Coupled with the Holy Spirit is the transcendent power of the pure love of Christ expressed with compassion, meekness, and purity.

Through that principle, I experienced a miracle in our mission. The miracle began when the Holy Ghost and the pure love of Christ came together in the midst of contention among some missionaries.

The phone rang in the mission home at 10:30 p.m.—a time when every missionary should be in bed. I knew something was wrong.

I answered and heard the anxious voice of a great zone leader. His words tumbled out: "Hello, President. I've got a problem. One of the senior couples is upset with two of the missionaries because something happened that didn't go right, and now the bishop's upset, and I'm the zone leader, and you told me to take care of it . . . and I don't know what to do. The senior couple is angry at me, and the elders don't think they were at fault, and the bishop's ready to call you. I just don't know what to do."

I could hear the anxiety in his voice, and I responded with what the Spirit prompted me to say: "Elder, let's pray tonight, and you call me tomorrow morning at 6:30, and then Heavenly Father by the power of the Holy Ghost will inspire us what to do."

Sure enough, just as the zone leader had predicted, the senior couple called me—even later that night—and said, "President Pinegar, we want to see you tomorrow morning." They anxiously explained their problem and expressed skepticism that a nineteen-year-old boy was capable of handling it.

"I have visited with the zone leader, and he will be prepared to handle all of your concerns," I said, trying to assure them. "Everything will be okay."

Instead of being assured, they were even more adamant about seeing me and felt no one could possibly understand how bad the situation was. They went on to describe the problem in detail from their perspective. They wanted me to know that everyone was upset, and they wanted me to handle it!

"I understand," I said. "The zone leader and I have visited, and he will take care of the problem." They were still upset. I simply thanked them for their concern and call and reassured them that all would be well.

The next morning, the zone leader called. It was clear that his anxiety was high and that contention was still rampant. He asked what he should do.

The Lord poured into my soul my answer to him through the power of the Holy Ghost. "Elder," I said, "first, have a kneeling prayer with everyone involved and pray that the Holy Spirit will be with them as they discuss the concerns of all involved. Pray that He will show them what to do, as in 2 Nephi 32:5. Pray that if their hearts are broken and contrite, and if they will be meek and lowly, the Lord will succor them in their pains and afflictions, as shown in Alma 7:11–12."

Buoyed and instructed by the Holy Ghost, I continued. "This will help them learn how the power of the Holy Ghost will fill us with the fruits of the Holy Spirit—love, joy, peace, longsuffering, gentleness, goodness, faith, meekness, and temperance, as described in Galatians 5:22–23. Ask them how they felt as you discussed these doctrines. They will begin to understand and appreciate that the Lord and the Holy Spirit can heal them.

"Finally, read and discuss Moroni 7:44–48, John 13:34–35, and Matthew 25:40. Then suggest in the spirit of love and charity that together you solve the problem as directed by the Holy Spirit." After giving the instruction I had been prompted to share, I felt peace and knew that everything would be okay. I knew love would abound.

Two hours later, the phone rang, and the zone leader reported what happened. "President, I just had the greatest day of my life. President, you never grow until you have a challenge. I was just sick to my stomach, but the Spirit of the Lord was so strong. We all cried, we all hugged, we all loved each other. We're going to do it. We made up. Things are right, and, President, the Lord healed us."

In that healing experience, that zone leader learned that the Holy Ghost reveals the truth from God the Father and our Savior Jesus Christ. He also learned that the power of the Lord's Atonement can heal us as we let the love of God into our hearts and as we express our feelings with the pure love of Christ. When the motive is love and we are meek, we can have visitations of the Holy Spirit:

> And the remission of sins bringeth meekness, and lowliness of heart; and *because of meekness and lowliness of heart cometh the visitation of the Holy Ghost*, which *Comforter filleth with hope and perfect love, which love endureth by diligence unto prayer*, until the end shall come, when all the saints shall dwell with God.[50]

Life is good when we live as directed by the Holy Spirit and follow our Savior in all that we do.

---

50   Moroni 8:26; emphasis added.

Chapter 2

PRAISE: THE APPROVAL AND COMPLIMENT NEEDED TO SUCCEED

You praise, inspire, and encourage everyone you can as an act of love. You seek to help others feel loved. You strengthen and bless those to whom you give PIE in a natural, spontaneous way—in small doses, like random acts of kindness.

The first step of PIE is praise. *Praise* is an expression of love that gives others the feeling of approval and acceptance for who they are and what they are doing.

When you give praise, you are giving and expressing love to others. The premise upon which praise is anchored comes from the deep-seated emotional need to be loved, appreciated, and approved. That is why it is important that psychological and emotional needs are met. When you genuinely praise others, you literally feed their spirit with love.

Sometimes praise—knowing that someone thinks they have done well and have the potential to do even better—is exactly what is needed to keep someone going. Never deny a prompting to praise.

Everyone can thrive on a simple compliment. Mark Twain once wrote, "I can live on a good compliment two weeks with nothing else to eat."[1] Remember that you can always give love through genuine and honest praise, and then hope that it will be well received.

While a single word of praise may be all someone needs, sometimes the same message needs to be sent over and over in a variety of ways—whether verbal, written, through a facial expression of approval, or a nod. Sometimes a simple smile will communicate praise.

Giving praise can help you become a new person of light. You become a giver. You become a lifter. You become a helper. You are continually seeking ways to bless others. As you praise others, you will literally "succor the weak, lift up the hands which hang down, and strengthen the feeble knees."[2]

Praising others is a mindset, not a complete overhaul of your life. It is a new vision. It is an exciting moment in life as you consider, *Who can I lift? How can I bless? Who seems a little down today?* You will find that this will become a joyful time of life as you lift and love others. You will fulfill the counsel given to Lyman Sherman: "Strengthen your brethren in all your conversation, in all your prayers, in all your exhortations, and in all your doings."[3]

People need approval. People need to feel accepted. People need to know they are all right. People need to know that they are of worth and can do meaningful things. Genuine praise and encouragement become some of the greatest motivating tools in the world. When you say something good about others, it blesses your life as well as theirs. You will have a better

---

1   Mark Twain, "Letter to Gertrude Natkin," March 2, 1906, http://www.twainquotes.com/Compliment.html.

2   D&C 81:5.

3   D&C 108:7.

relationship with others, and everyone involved will find joy in their work.

While serving as president of the Provo Missionary Training Center, I had a prompting to help the missionaries with PIE. I had little cards made and distributed them to the teachers, branch presidents, and others. I asked each of them to fill out the card concerning a specific missionary who had done well or performed some special act of goodness. When the cards were turned in to my office, I wrote the missionary a personal letter including the praise contained in the little card—and I also sent a copy of the letter to the missionary's parents. It became a great strengthening force in the lives of several hundred missionaries.

I relate that experience to ask that you never doubt the power of praise. It can make the difference in the life of another that may subsequently ripple to many others.

President Howard W. Hunter said, "We enjoy life when we have the ability to praise others for their good works. George Matthew Adams said, 'He who praises another enriches himself far more than he does the one praised. To praise is an investment in happiness. . . . The poorest human being has something to give that the richest cannot buy.'"[4]

Consider the following five points when offering praise:[5]

WHEN TO PRAISE

- *Do It without Delay*—Procrastinated praise and delayed encouragement lose their power. Do it in a timely manner, while it is still fresh in your mind.

4 "Gifts That Money Cannot Buy" (Brigham Young University devotional, April 26, 1961), 3, speeches.byu.edu.

5 Adapted from Ed J. Pinegar and Richard J. Allen, *Living by the Word* (American Fork, UT: Covenant Communications, 2005), 278–80.

- *Do It Each Day*—Praise or encourage someone honestly and openly every day. Do it regularly. Make it a habit.
- *Do It When People Are Sad or Distraught*—Elder Neal A. Maxwell said, "So often we can serve by bathing the wounded and bruised egos of others in the warm waters of deserved commendation."[6]

HOW TO PRAISE

- *Be Specific*—Identify the precise behavior or result that has elicited your appreciation and refer to it specifically.
- *Do It with Enthusiasm*—It's not always what you say, but how you say it that conveys your true feelings.
- *Be Genuine*—True praise is never maudlin or affected in any way; it is always sincere and honest.
- *Use Variety*—Spoken words are effective, but there are other ways that can work just as well: an appropriate small gift, a helpful news clipping, a text, an email, or a favor returned can all be effective.
- *Do It with Gratitude*—Always offer praise in a spirit of gratitude. And remember to receive praise from others with graciousness and appreciation. Accept praise from others as a genuine gift, just as you want others to receive your praise.

WHAT TO PRAISE

- *Small and Great Things*—Praise small things, not just great achievements. Praise improvements, courage, and the efforts that go into those things.

---

6 *The Neal A. Maxwell Quote Book*, ed. Cory H. Maxwell (Salt Lake City: Bookcraft, 1997), 260.

WHERE TO PRAISE

- *In Public and in Private*—Don't hesitate to give praise in public, as long as it doesn't embarrass the person.

WHO TO PRAISE

- *Your Spouse*—We often forget to give encouragement to the one closest to us. Don't take the one so dear to you for granted.
- *Especially Children*—Remember that children grow and improve much faster with praise than with criticism.
- *Even Your "Enemies"*—There is good in everyone. It will often amaze you what effect genuine praise—direct or indirect—will have on those you consider not entirely your friends.
- *Everyone*—Praise strangers as well as friends. Look for something good about everyone with whom you come in contact.
- *Heavenly Father*—Let God, "from whom all blessings flow,"[7] also have your daily praise and thanks.

This may seem like a recipe or list of things to do, but as you read and reread, you will come to realize that these are essential reminders for helping others have a happy and successful life. Helping others through honest, genuine praise brings joy to your soul and to the souls of others. Eyes will sparkle. Hearts will leap with joy. People will have a little bounce in their step. And yes, life will be better.

Expressing thanksgiving and gratitude as a form of praise brings so much joy to the receiver as well as the giver. As you look to see the good in others, you will live life on a higher and holier plain. We surely should seek after praiseworthy

---

7 "Praise God, from Whom All Blessings Flow," *Hymns*, no. 242.

things and bring joy to others as we practice the principle of praise. Expressing honest, genuine praise can change the soul.

Consider the following reminders that may provide additional insights about the principle of praise:

- Praising and thanking Heavenly Father brings Him into your life through mighty and humble prayers. Praising God through prayer or hymns is a form of worship[8] that is an expression of your love of God.

- Praising God through prayer is demonstrated by Nephi and Ammon. Read Nephi's psalm in 2 Nephi 4:17–35. Also read Ammon's expressions of gratitude to the Lord in Alma 26 for all the Lord had helped him and his brothers do in bringing thousands of Lamanites into the fold of Christ.

- To enter the Lord's holy temple, you need to be in the spirit of thanksgiving and praise: "Enter into his gates with thanksgiving, and into his courts with praise: be thankful unto him, and bless his name."[9]

- Praise should be given freely to those you teach and serve as you help them along their way.

- Praise is a natural expression of love to those who seek to follow Christ and help others.

- Praise reinforces your hope and your actions to carry on with confidence and resilience.

- Praise gives the receiver an inner power to know they are esteemed in the eyes of others. When they notice your efforts and receive your kindness, they become empowered to do better.

---

8 See Alma 33:3.
9 Psalm 100:4.

- When giving praise, you lose yourself in helping others be their best because you live outside yourself with the pure love of Christ. You experience joy in the success of others.
- Comparison and competition are swept away when you express love with PIE.
- Receiving praise brings light and a positive feeling for what you are doing. You know that your efforts are worthwhile, and you are making a difference because of who you are and what you do. There is *no* self-defeating attitude or negativism in your attitude. Receiving praise in meekness and humility empowers you to do even better.
- The manner in which you give praise often determines its effectiveness in lifting the receiver. Praise must be given with a genuine attitude of benevolence, with no thought of receiving reciprocation, and it must be motivated by love and a desire to bless and help others who are worthy of your praise.
- Often, recipients are overcome by your praise, and they have a hard time receiving it—especially if they haven't received praise very much in their lives. You must be authentic and sincere, and you must be patient and understanding if it seems difficult for them to accept.
- Learn to praise often whenever you observe someone's effort. When you praise often, it will become a part of your natural behavior. Praising others will simply be who you are and what you do; you will always be looking for the good, even when good is hard to find.
- Praise can lift strangers, coworkers, family members, and all those with whom you come into contact. The good you do in praising someone cascades into other lives through your praise.

- Think of the blessings of being a praise-oriented person— it takes only a moment in time. You can write a note of praise in one or two minutes, and that small investment of time will make the recipients happy. And you will help them continue to improve in doing whatever you praised them for. And that's not all: you'll feel happy too.

- Praising others is a form of keeping the second great commandment and brings joy to the Savior, for He said, "And the King shall answer and say unto them, Verily I say unto you, Inasmuch as ye have done it unto one of the least of these my brethren, ye have done it unto me."[10]

- Proverbs teaches us to not withhold a good word of praise to the deserving: "Withhold not good from them to whom it is due, when it is in the power of thine hand to do it."[11]

- A good opportunity to praise others occurs around the dinner table for someone's birthday and for Easter, Thanksgiving, Christmas, and any special day on which you want to have a wonderful time. You can go around the table taking turns complimenting and praising everyone, each one at a time. It becomes a feast of spiritual enlightenment and rejuvenation. Everyone feels good when praising and complimenting others.

- Your relationships deepen when you give and receive praise.

- When you think of others and ponder on their goodness, praise will naturally flow from you.

---

10   Matthew 25:40.
11   Proverbs 3:27.

- Next time you go grocery shopping, look for opportunities to express gratitude and appreciation for the help you receive. "Thank you." "You are so kind." "Could you tell me what aisle the pies are on? . . . Thank you!" Shopping becomes a time of expressing love.

Chapter 3

INSPIRATION: THE SUPERNAL EXPRESSION
OF THE HOLY GHOST

Teaching, presenting, and giving instruction by the power of the Holy Ghost is the greatest power whereby you can inspire others to do better and be better. To teach is not only a great calling and opportunity; it carries with it an even greater responsibility: "And the Spirit shall be given unto you by the prayer of faith; and if ye receive not the Spirit ye shall not teach."[1]

When teaching, you become responsible for those you teach. Jacob explains:

> And we did magnify our office unto the Lord, taking upon us the responsibility, answering the sins of the people upon our own heads if we did not teach them the word of God with all diligence; wherefore, by laboring with our might their blood might not come upon our garments; otherwise their blood would come upon our garments, and we would not be found spotless at the last day.[2]

---

1   D&C 42:14.
2   Jacob 1:19.

The act of teaching has great potential for inspiring others and influencing their growth. Henry Adams said, "A teacher affects eternity; he can never tell where his influence stops."[3]

Whether by precept or example, a skillful teacher creates an atmosphere of learning and inspires change and improvement. For good or ill, all of us are teachers because invariably someone is always watching or listening. Great teachers have the power, the skills, and the opportunity to make a difference in others' lives and in society.

INSPIRING THOSE YOU LOVE AND TEACH

Consider the following six points for inspiring those you love and teach. They will help you receive the power of the Holy Ghost, whether in a formal teaching situation or, more often, in day-to-day relationships:

1. **An effective teacher teaches from the heart, as directed by the power of the Holy Ghost.**
    *   *Believe what you teach*—an effective teacher believes what he or she is teaching and presents it with conviction. Knowing what to teach and why you teach it is taught by the power of the Holy Ghost.
2. **An effective teacher is motivated by love and respect.**
    *   *The key ingredient is love*—above all other qualities, an effective teacher has a generous measure of love for the learner.
    *   *Blend love with respect*—a part of showing love is showing respect. An effective teacher treats those he or she seeks to inspire with dignity and encouragement.

---

3   *The Education of Henry Adams*, ch. 20. (1907), https://www.oxfordreference.com/view/10.1093/acref/9780191843730.001.0001/q-oro-ed5-00000038.

Meekness and humility will empower you to teach with the power of the Holy Ghost.

3. **An effective teacher is visionary.**

    *   *Focus on the potential*—an effective teacher sees less of what is and more of what might be. Above all, a good teacher has confidence in the outcome of the teaching process because the student can catch the vision of his or her own future only when the teacher clearly sees the potential of the student.

    *   *Open the eyes of those you seek to teach*—an effective teacher illuminates new pathways, better opportunities to seek growth, and better knowledge for living and learning.

    *   *Illuminate the understanding*—one key to effective teaching is to ensure that learners understand the information and see its value. When they understand, they can appreciate. When appreciation is felt, gratitude swells within their very soul, and they will have a desire to change and do good. Gratitude improves attitudes, increases spirituality, and becomes a catalyst for change.

4. **An effective teacher is exemplary of the learning process.**

    *   *Be diligent*—an effective teacher demonstrates the qualities of hard work, persistence, and the determination to excel in order to model the very process by which those they teach can come to the knowledge of the truth. Learners need to take responsibility for their learning. This is a giant step in living the gospel of Jesus Christ.

    *   *Know the needs of those you teach*—an effective teacher knows the needs, concerns, strengths, and desires of

those they teach. When you help fulfill the needs of others, they will be full of gratitude for what you do.

- *Earn their trust*—an effective teacher establishes relationships of trust and credibility with those they teach.
- *Be meek and humble*—an effective teacher is meek and humble, ever willing to confess that he or she is also a student who must continue to learn each day to increase in the knowledge of the truth.
- *Be balanced*—an effective teacher demonstrates an interest in the well-being of the learner in all aspects of the learner's life.

5. **An effective teacher builds an environment for optimal growth.**
   - *Cultivate a genuine locus of learning*—create an appealing atmosphere for learning and change. This does not refer to the classroom or to the physical space as much as to the framework for learning— the vision, the relationships, the opportunities, the excitement, and the encouragement.
   - *Focus on desire*—when you create the desire to learn, the hardest step in the learning process has been taken. Desire is the fuel for learning. "Experience teaches only the teachable," counseled Aldous Huxley.[4]
   - *Listen*—a humble teacher listens. This skill allows the teacher to discern the needs, strengths, and potential of the individual. One anonymous writer said, "Until you know how they feel, think, and believe, you cannot teach with power."

4 "Quote by Aldous Huxley," *Goodreads*, https://www.goodreads.com/quotes/87841-experience-teaches-only-the-teachable.

- *Teach by the power of the Holy Spirit*—teach efficiently and effectively. When the heart is touched, the spirit within begins to change.
- *Use action*—involve those you teach in the teaching process. Discovery learning is very powerful.
- *Use high energy*—make learning fun and exciting. Learning can be one of the great adventures of life.
- *Encourage reach*—help those you teach stretch beyond their level. This inspires creativity and discovery.
- *Be gracious and complimentary*—give praise often, inspire with the Spirit, and encourage learners regularly.
- *Be creative*—be resourceful and innovative. No legitimate option for learning should be left unattended and unapplied where it might assist those you teach to have the "aha" moments needed for true discovery learning.

6. **An effective teacher is patient.**
   - *Never give up*—be patient. Some learners grasp concepts immediately; others take more time. You cannot force a young tree to grow up any faster than nature has provided for its growth. But you can continually nourish it, prune it in wisdom, and provide an environment where it can rise to fulfill its destiny.
   - *Watch for the straggler*—encourage those who struggle and fall behind. Look for signs of discouragement. Shore up the weak and instill hope in the fearful with constant encouragement.
   - *Start in the family*—parents have been commanded to "teach their children to pray, and to walk uprightly

before the Lord," or else "the sin be upon the heads of the parents."[5]

As you can see, teaching is not just about imparting information, but also about inspiring and motivating others to do better and be better. Surely teaching by the power of the Holy Ghost is the greatest influence for good. So how do you ensure that you inspire and motivate those you teach? You teach through the power of the Holy Ghost.

The ability to help others feel the presence and power of the Holy Ghost will inspire and motivate the learner to greater heights and spirituality:

> And now, verily, verily, I say unto thee, put your trust in that Spirit which leadeth to do good—yea, to do justly, to walk humbly, to judge righteously; and this is my Spirit.
>
> Verily, verily, I say unto you, I will impart unto you of my Spirit, which shall enlighten your mind, which shall fill your soul with joy.[6]

INSPIRATION AND MOTIVATION BY THE POWER OF THE HOLY GHOST

Inspiration affects the mind and heart. Responding to that power, one becomes enthused, enlivened, aroused, and even provoked to greater heights. It truly prompts us to be better. This is the power of the Holy Ghost. The effect depends upon the faith of both the giver and the receiver of the word of God. When one feels a need for something, the power to be inspired is greatly enhanced.

---

5 D&C 68:25–28.
6 D&C 11:12–13.

As you look for ways to inspire and motivate those you serve, here are some things to remember about how to do so by the power of the Holy Ghost:

1. **Help Others Gain the Vision of What You Are Helping Them to Learn**
   - *Be principle-based*—seek to inspire with the knowledge of the truth and the principles of the gospel of Jesus Christ. Remember, teachings and principles understood and appreciated will cause one to feel gratitude for what they have learned. Gratitude is a catalyst to motivate and inspire a change of heart and mind.
   - *See from a higher perspective*—a meaningful vision of the covenant path is a greater banner for action. A true perspective will inspire and motivate people to press onward to achieve worthy goals.

2. **Preparing Is the Key to Receiving Inspiration to Inspire and Motivate Others**
   - *Be exemplary*—to inspire and motivate others in any given area, you need to be credible and exemplary in that area. You need to be a genuine example of what is being taught and conveyed by inspiration.
   - *Be enthusiastic*—in attempting to inspire others, you need to be "on fire" yourself so that you radiate the feelings of the heart.

3. **Understanding Brings Appreciation, Which Leads to Gratitude—the Catalyst for Change**
   - *Discern needs*—do whatever you can to understand the needs of those you are trying to help. Needs become great motivators. Pain makes one more receptive to new ideas for change. The guilt-ridden are often more

susceptible to spiritual inspiration. Those with health problems are more open to promising solutions. Any untenable situation makes one more easily motivated. Be sensitive to deep needs.

- *Listen*—to inspire people, be aware of what they care about. When you listen and strive to understand, they will know you care. Then you can more readily inspire and motivate. Similarly, to receive inspiration and motivation, you need to be a good listener who is easily entreated by the Holy Ghost.

4. **Create a Plan to Succeed**
   - *Explain benefits and blessings*—provide those you are trying to help with an incentive to do something. Make clear the benefits of the action. If a person clearly understands the advantages to be had through the action, then he or she will more readily do it. By providing incentive, you can touch the hearts of people and inspire them to action. The Lord always makes clear the promised blessings to help us stay on the covenant path.
   - *Praise*—be an effective cheerleader. Point out the milestones reached. Give praise where deserved.
   - *Foster teamwork*—"You can do it!" is powerful, but "Let's do it!" is often even more powerful. Unity empowers a team or group if they have agreed-upon values.
   - *Love*—you will have the greatest influence on those who know you love them. Let people know you truly care for them and express it appropriately.

5. **Strive for Personal Inspiration and Motivation**
   - *Seek personal inspiration*—you will be most effective in helping others if you rely on personal inspiration. That inspiration can come as a prompting from the Holy Ghost as you seek counsel from Heavenly Father.
   - *Meditate and ponder*—as you study things out and think on those things of importance, you can have inspiration as to what to do—and you can teach others to do the same. Both Nephi and President Joseph F. Smith give us powerful examples of meditating and pondering prior to revelations.[7]
   - *Seek counsel and advice*—as you seek counsel though prayer or from other trusted leaders, you can receive new perspectives and approaches that can enlighten your mind and motivate you to greater heights. In turn, you can help others to experience the same benefits.

BE OF GOOD CHEER—YOU CAN LIFT OTHERS[8]

One of our callings in the Church is to cheer each other up, buoy each other up, and help pump up each other's faith and hope. The gateway to your inspiration for that mission is to be of good cheer. There are times that might seem difficult. Consider the following examples:

1. *When you feel inadequate.* That's how Thomas Marsh, President of the Quorum of the Twelve, must have felt in 1837:

---

7 See 1 Nephi 11:1–2; D&C 138:1–4, 11.
8 My good friend Richard J. Allen was kind enough to provide this section on being of good cheer.

> Verily I say unto you, there have been some
> few things in thine heart and with thee with
> which I, the Lord, was not well pleased.
>
> Nevertheless, inasmuch as thou hast abased
> thyself thou shalt be exalted; therefore, all
> thy sins are forgiven thee.
>
> Let thy heart be of good cheer before my
> face; and thou shalt bear record of my name,
> not only unto the Gentiles, but also unto
> the Jews; and thou shalt send forth my word
> unto the ends of the earth.[9]

Is that not a reason to be of good cheer? Would you be of good cheer if you knew your sins were forgiven and you were therefore worthy of spiritual responsibilities in the service of others?

2. *When your faith is tested.* Remember the contemporaries of Nephi after the prophecy of Samuel and how anxious they were that the sign of the coming of the Lord had not been given? What did Nephi do?

> And it came to pass that he cried mightily
> unto the Lord all that day; and behold, the
> voice of the Lord came unto him, saying:
>
> Lift up your head and be of good cheer;
> for behold, the time is at hand, and on this
> night shall the sign be given, and on the
> morrow come I into the world, to show unto
> the world that I will fulfill all that which I

---

9   D&C 112:2–4.

have caused to be spoken by the mouth of
my holy prophets.[10]

Why should they be of good cheer? Because the Redeemer
was to become Emmanuel—*God with us*. He will fulfill all His
promises. Is it easy for you to be of good cheer knowing that
the Savior will fulfill all His promises to you?

3. *When you feel weak or ill.* Here's a scripture to remember
    when you are ailing: "And, behold, they brought to him
    a man sick of the palsy, lying on a bed: and Jesus seeing
    their faith said unto the sick of the palsy; Son, be of good
    cheer; thy sins are forgiven thee. . . . Arise, take up thy
    bed, and go unto thine house."[11] And he was healed.
    Why should he be of good cheer? He was healed—both
    physically and spiritually. What a great blessing! We can
    also feel the strength of the Spirit that helps us experience
    enduring cheer.

4. *When you face a daunting challenge.* When attacked by the
    enemy, Ammon told the king's servants, "My brethren, be
    of good cheer and let us go in search of the flocks, and we
    will gather them together and bring them back unto the
    place of water; and thus we will preserve the flocks unto
    the king."[12] Why should they be of good cheer? Because
    a prophet-warrior was leading them in a plan for solving
    their problem. They could follow a prophet. Does it cause
    you to be of good cheer to know that a prophet of God is
    leading you (and all of us) in solving our problems?

---

10   3 Nephi 1:12–13.
11   Matthew 9:2, 6.
12   Alma 17:31.

5. *When you are called upon to bear testimony before the world.* When the Prophet Joseph Smith inquired of the Lord regarding the elders of the Church in 1831, he received the following revelation:

> And this is the ensample unto them, that they shall speak as they are moved upon by the Holy Ghost.
>
> And whatsoever they shall speak when moved upon by the Holy Ghost shall be scripture, shall be the will of the Lord, shall be the mind of the Lord, shall be the word of the Lord, shall be the voice of the Lord, and the power of God unto salvation.
>
> Behold, this is the promise of the Lord unto you, O ye my servants.
>
> Wherefore, be of good cheer, and do not fear, for I the Lord am with you, and will stand by you; and ye shall bear record of me, even Jesus Christ, that I am the Son of the living God, that I was, that I am, and that I am to come.[13]

Why would you be of good cheer when you are called on to testify in circumstances that are uncomfortable or even frightening? Because you can be worthy of inspiration, which means the Spirit is doing the talking.

6. *When you are persecuted for the sake of the gospel.* Consider an incident when Paul was imprisoned for being valiant in the faith:

13 D&C 68:3–6.

> And the night following the Lord stood by
> him (in prison) and said, Be of good cheer,
> Paul: for as thou hast testified of me in
> Jerusalem, so must thou bear witness also
> at Rome.[14]

How can you be of good cheer when undergoing persecution? Because, like Paul, your mission is not yet finished—and you, like Paul, will be preserved to complete it.

Cheerfulness is the eternal fruit of a life of forgiveness. If you are faithful and obedient, the Lord fulfills His promises. You can receive great spiritual wealth. The Lord will heal your spirit and often your physical impairments. The Holy Spirit will tell you what to say and do. You can follow the prophets.

The Savior is in charge during the storms of life. There is safety in the Lord. You will be preserved until your mission is completed. The Lord has overcome the world, and He always provides the way for you and all of us to be of good cheer.

---

14   Acts 23:11.

Chapter 4
ENCOURAGEMENT: THE CONTINUED
REINFORCEMENT FOR GROWTH

GIVING AND EXPRESSING ENCOURAGEMENT IS the concluding ingredient in PIE. Without consistent and genuine encouragement, people often lose their impetus and slowly come to a sad halt in their growth. Encouragement is the lifeblood to the mind and heart just as air and water are to the body. Without encouragement, all of us perish.

A friend of mine recently attended a large multidistrict teacher training. The importance of encouraging students was heavily emphasized as a way to positively influence student achievement that is within a teacher's control. The effectiveness of encouragement is not limited to the classroom, however. Think about this quote by successful businessman Charles M. Schwab: "I consider my ability to arouse enthusiasm among my people . . . the greatest asset I possess, and the way to develop the best that is in a person is by appreciation and encouragement. There is nothing else that so kills the ambitions of a person as criticisms from superiors."[1] Encouragement is how we build others.

---

1   Charles Schwab, quoted in Dale Carnegie, *How to Win Friends and Influence People* (New York: Pocket Books, 1936), 23.

Take a moment to think of all the tender mercies showered on you from Heavenly Father and our Savior.[2] Those tender mercies are reminders of the constant encouragement you are given by Heavenly Father and our Savior.

President Gordon B. Hinckley has said this about our need to encourage others:

> We have such an obligation to those who are baptized into the Church. We cannot neglect them. We cannot leave them to stand alone. They need help as they become accustomed to the ways and culture of this Church. And it is our great blessing and opportunity to afford that help. . . . A warm smile, a friendly handshake, an encouraging word will do wonders.[3]

Encouragement is the process or act of giving confidence and courage to help others pursue their goals and meet the tasks that lie ahead. Your encouraging words and acts can give them the incentive and the desire to act. Encouragement can even inspire them toward heroic levels of performance. It truly incites and promotes one to greater heights.

You never know when your encouraging word will make the difference in one's life—life-changing moments may come at any time. An encouraging word and continued support will always help another, as this oft-told story illustrates in a dramatic way:

---

2 See Moroni 10:3.

3 "Inspirational Thoughts," *Ensign*, October 2003.

One day, when I was a freshman in high school, I saw a kid from my class was walking home from school. His name was Kyle. It looked like he was carrying all of his books. I thought to myself, "Why would anyone bring home all his books on a Friday? He must really be a nerd." I had quite a weekend planned (parties and a football game with my friend tomorrow afternoon), so I shrugged my shoulders and went on. As I was walking, I saw a bunch of kids running toward him. They ran at him, knocking all his books out of his arms and tripping him so he landed in the dirt. His glasses went flying, and I saw them land in the grass about ten feet from him. He looked up and I saw this terrible sadness in his eyes. My heart went out to him. So, I jogged over to him and as he crawled around looking for his glasses, I saw a tear in his eye.

As I handed him his glasses, I said, "Those guys are jerks. They really should get lives." He looked at me and said, "Hey thanks!" There was a big smile on his face. It was one of those smiles that showed real gratitude.

I helped him pick up his books and asked him where he lived. As it turned out, he lived near me, so I asked him why I had never seen him before. He said he had gone to private school before now. I would have never hung out with a private school kid before.

We talked all the way home, and I carried his books. He turned out to be a pretty cool kid. I asked him if he wanted to play football on Saturday with me and my friends. He said yes. We hung all weekend, and the more I got to know Kyle, the more I liked him. And my friends thought the same of him.

Monday morning came, and there was Kyle with the huge stack of books again. I stopped him and said, ". . . boy, you are gonna really build some serious muscles with this pile of books every day!" He just laughed and handed me half the books. Over the next four years, Kyle and I became best friends.

When we were seniors, we began to think about college. Kyle decided on Georgetown, and I was going to Duke. I knew that we would always be friends, that the miles would never be a problem. He was going to be a doctor, and I was going for business on a football scholarship. Kyle was valedictorian of our class.

I teased him all the time about being a nerd. He had to prepare a speech for graduation. I was so glad it wasn't me having to get up there and speak.

Graduation day, I saw Kyle. He looked great. He was one of those guys that really found himself during high school. He filled out and actually looked good in glasses. He had more dates than me and all the girls loved him! Boy, sometimes I was jealous.

Today was one of those days. I could see that he was nervous about his speech. So, I smacked him on the back and said, "Hey, big guy, you'll be great!" He looked at me with one of those looks (the really grateful one) and smiled.

"Thanks," he said.

As he started his speech, he cleared his throat, and began. "Graduation is a time to thank those who helped you make it through those tough years. Your parents, your teachers, your siblings, maybe a coach . . . but mostly your friends. I am here to tell all of you that being a friend to someone is the best gift you can give them. I am going to tell you a story." I just looked at my friend with disbelief as he told the story of the first day we met. He had planned to kill himself over the weekend. He talked of how he had cleaned out his locker so his Mom wouldn't have to do it later and was carrying his stuff home. He looked hard at me and gave me a little smile. "Thankfully, I was saved. My friend saved me from doing the unspeakable." I heard the gasp go through the crowd as this handsome, popular boy told us all about his weakest moment.

I saw his mom and dad looking at me and smiling that same grateful smile. Not until that moment did I realize its depth. Never underestimate the power of your actions.

With one small gesture you can change a person's life. For better or for worse. God puts us all in each other's lives to impact one another in some way. Look for God in others.[4]

When I read this story, I teared up and realized the power of love that never wavered and that is expressed with time, concern, compassion, praise, friendship, and encouragement.

THE POWER OF ENCOURAGEMENT

Encouragement brings reassurance and reinforcement into others' lives as well as your own. Encouragement is uplifting and has staying power. It brightens both the giver and those who choose to receive it. It gives hope for the day ahead and even enhances physiological and emotional health. And there's nothing complicated or mysterious about it: everyone can learn to be encouraging.

Encouraging others brings with it a whole host of blessings within the gospel of Jesus Christ, including the following:

- *Common vision*—you help cultivate a new attitude of harmony toward the gospel of Jesus Christ and following our Savior Jesus Christ.

---

4   Jack Canfield and Mark Victor Hansen, *Chicken Soup for the Soul* (Deerfield Beach, FL: Health Communications, 1993), 35–36.

- *Understanding*—you help others gain knowledge, which leads them to understanding and appreciating the Lord and His gospel.
- *Hope*—you help supply the nutrients of hope and positive support that increase the faith of others and help them stay the course on the covenant path.
- *Self-worth and self-esteem*—as you encourage others, your own self-worth and self-esteem increase, as do theirs; you help them understand their divine nature and their divine potential.
- *Love*—with encouragement comes the empowerment of love, the greatest motive for change.
- *Enthusiasm*—you bring to the relationship the sunshine of enthusiasm and energy.
- *The Holy Ghost*—your encouragement motivates others to seek the companionship of the Holy Ghost, who is a revelator and a motivator.[5]
- *Legacy*—you help those you encourage have a renewed confidence and resilience. Your encouragement can help them see who they are and what they can truly become. Self-doubt flees from their minds.

Encouragement can enhance our relationship with others and with Heavenly Father, our Savior Jesus Christ, and the Holy Ghost. Paul said it this way: "But he that prophesieth speaketh unto men to edification, and exhortation, and comfort."[6] You can help others get even more encouragement by urging them to diligently study the scriptures, which are filled with encouragement from the Lord Jesus Christ, the Holy Ghost, and the prophets.

---

5   See 2 Nephi 32:5; D&C 11:12–13.

6   1 Corinthians 14:3.

As you encourage, you build trust, kindness, respect, loyalty, support, and a sense of care for each other—all good reasons to give encouragement. Those receiving encouragement will be empowered, and they will feel renewed and refreshed. As you embrace expressions of love by sharing PIE, you are creating a new way to look at life and a new way to live.

As a young boy, I had a strong desire to play basketball. I thought basketball was the greatest, and I thought playing basketball for Brigham Young University would be a dream come true.

Unfortunately, my high school basketball coach didn't think I was good enough to make the sophomore team as a ninth grader. Two of my classmates did make the team, and I was devastated. The following year, I did make the team, and though I started some games, I was never a dominant player. During my junior year in high school, I was on the varsity team, and I was about the eighth man. So again, I was played sparingly.

One day, as we started the season in my senior year, the new coach, Don Snow, called me into his office and said to me, "Ed, you are going to be a great ball player. You will be my starting center and captain of the team. You are going to be a strong leader and player. I'll show you how." With praise like that, I just knew I'd be a success on the court. Coach Snow was gifted at serving PIE to his players, and it paid off.

We worked hard. I listened to my new coach and wanted to make him proud. That year, our team took second place in the state tournament. I was voted All-State, and I led the region in scoring. Best of all, I was offered a scholarship to Brigham Young University, where I played ball for the legendary coach

Stan Watts. We had some great success and some wonderful victories. Life really was great—and it all started with, "Ed, you are going to be a great ball player." I am a product of a great coach who gave me PIE.

Encouragement is the ongoing expression of love that motivates others to keep trying to be their best. It feeds the soul with small doses of hope, increases their faith, and gives them additional strength and resilience. It continually helps build your relationships with those you encourage. Never doubt the power of a kind, supporting word to those with whom you associate.

The fruits of encouragement fulfill the wonderful counsel in Proverbs: "The liberal soul shall be made fat: and he that watereth shall be watered also himself."[7] In other words, people who are generous with compliments and who encourage others are rewarded with a refreshing, revitalizing, and energizing of the soul—as are the people who are encouraged. Proverbs also tells us, "Pleasant words are as an honeycomb, sweet to the soul, and health to the bones."[8] The power to bless one another is limitless if you are willing and able to realize the power within you to praise, inspire, and encourage.

I am also the product of my sweet mother's PIE. Ringing in my ears to this day are the words of my angel mother: "You are such a good boy; just be good." The result of her words to me was a lifelong quest to be a good boy and to please my mama. Little did I realize my widowed mother was always serving me PIE through her consistent praise, inspiration, and

---

7 Proverbs 11:25.
8 Proverbs 16:24.

encouragement for fifty-two years following the death of my father. Her words changed my life.

You can be that kind of influence in the lives of others as you look for ways to encourage:

- If you see anything lovely or of good report, tell someone about it. You will be praising God and the one who was involved with the project.
- When served by any clerk or store employee, give that person an encouraging word. Tell the manager too.
- When you get some good advice, thank the person who gave it to you, and the chain of encouragement will continue.
- Many moments throughout the day will bring you opportunities to encourage someone in a special way.

The scriptures are filled to the brim with words of encouragement for us during our mortal journeys here on earth. I've compiled some of my favorite examples of scriptural PIE. I urge you to ponder these encouraging words from the scriptures that reflect the love of God and our Savior Jesus Christ:

Proverbs 3:5–6: "Trust in the Lord with all thine heart; and lean not unto thine own understanding. In all thy ways acknowledge him, and he shall direct thy paths."

Psalm 55:22: "Cast thy burden upon the Lord, and he shall sustain thee: he shall never suffer the righteous to be moved."

Luke 22:32: "But I have prayed for thee, that thy faith fail not: and when thou art converted, strengthen thy brethren."

D&C 108:7: "Therefore, strengthen your brethren in all your conversation, in all your prayers, in all your exhortations, and in all your doings."

D&C 81:5–6: "Wherefore, be faithful; stand in the office which I have appointed unto you; succor the weak, lift up the hands which hang down, and strengthen the feeble knees. And if thou art faithful unto the end thou shalt have a crown of immortality, and eternal life in the mansions which I have prepared in the house of my Father."

I read these words and I just know life will be wonderful. Love will abound. As we generously share PIE with all those around us, we can't help but be filled in return, and the love of God will bring us joy and happiness.

Chapter 5
CREATING AN ENVIRONMENT FOR GROWTH AND SUCCESS

YOU CAN GREATLY ASSIST OTHERS by having them understand and appreciate what needs to happen in order for them to grow and have a measure of success. Take the time to help those you are assisting understand and appreciate the following five principles of success that each individual needs to know and do in order to achieve his or her goals.

FIVE PRINCIPLES OF SUCCESS

1. Vision—what do they want to become? Do they have a plan and goals that reflect that vision?
2. Desire—do they have a great desire to achieve that vision? Will they stick to the plan and goals they have set?
3. Preparation—are they willing to pay the price required to accomplish their goal?
4. Enthusiasm—is there a fire within them that will carry them through? The word *enthusiasm* in Greek refers to having "God within us." Our Savior had God with Him when He accomplished the good He did.[1]

---

1   See Acts 10:38.

5. Dedication—will they have the diligence and commitment required to achieve their goals?

A person who wants to have success needs these five elements to stay focused on plans and goals. Help those you are serving reflect on these five principles periodically as they work toward their goals.

SIX PRINCIPLES TO HELP OTHERS CHANGE

When working with those you serve, including your own children, it's critical that you create an environment for growth and change. Listed below are six principles you need to understand and appreciate so you can help others grow and change.

1. **Gain their respect and trust.** Develop a personal relationship of trust; trust is vital in helping others change. Work toward respect for each other and for you as their teacher/leader/friend. Remember that those expressing love through PIE need to be respected by the receivers of that love. When you give and receive love through expressions of PIE, respect develops, and relationships are strengthened and increased between the giver and receiver.

2. **Help them feel a need to change.** We need to understand the needs of others and help them feel the genuine need to change. Increased desires to do better and be better are enhanced as one receives praise, inspiration, and encouragement from others—the elements that propel one to change for the better.

3. **Help them feel increased self-esteem.** An appreciation and respect for oneself—a healthy self-esteem—is essential for positive change. Those who want to make genuine change

need to know that they are the children of God the Father and that they have a divine heritage and purpose here on earth. Giving genuine PIE to others always increases their self-esteem, self-worth, self-confidence, and the ability to rise every time they fall. Encouragement enhances the resilience—the ability to recover fully from any adversity—deep within each of us until resilience becomes part of who we are.

4. **Give them information to act on and specific things to do.** It is difficult to inspire someone to change with vague concepts and suggestions. As well-meaning as exhortations of "invite the Spirit into your life" might be, it doesn't exactly tell them *how* to make that change. Rather, inspire them to take specific action or make specific changes, such as "begin your day with a prayer so the Spirit is with you throughout your day." But remember, encouraging people to do any task requires motivation—and the strongest motivation is love. While encouraging specific actions provides them with a clear course forward, it is your inspired words of praise, inspiration, and encouragement—given in love—that will help them achieve those specific goals.

5. **Help them create their value system.** Help those you serve understand and appreciate a value system built on the gospel of Jesus Christ. People value what they love. Their true value system is where their heart is, as the Lord reminded us: "For where your treasure is, there will your heart be also."[2] If they are enduring and wholesome, values lead to change for the better. Small doses of genuine PIE will help others stay the course of their value system

2   Matthew 6:21.

because they know there is someone who understands their values and thinks they are doing well upholding them.

6. **Help them sustain their commitment to change.** Help those you serve keep their commitment to change. Remind them that we all express our love for God by keeping His commandments—something that requires commitment. Their commitment to the task of change is increased when they know there is someone who thinks they are doing great and who uses praise, inspiration, and encouragement to express confidence that they can achieve their goals.

Let's consider each of these elements of change in more detail.

GAIN THEIR RESPECT AND TRUST

When people understand that you respect, love, and trust them, they are more willing to yield to your persuasion and encouragement.

To *respect* means to regard highly, to show consideration for, to honor or esteem, to revere and hallow, to think much of, to look up to, and to pay careful attention to. When people respect you, your power to influence them is greatly increased because they listen to people they respect and trust.

Relationships of *trust* are forged and strengthened as your credibility is increased through mutual respect. Your relationship with others is enhanced when you care about what they care about. These common interests and concerns sustain a relationship and an environment in which you can influence and bless them.

Gaining respect and love for those with whom you work and for whom you have responsibility is vital for a relationship of trust. Consider some of the following principles and ideas for building respect and trust:

- Let them know you love them.
- Live the standards you teach.
- Be humble and meek.
- Develop suitable service skills.
- Respect others for who they are and for who they can become.

To teach or lead others, you need to have deep respect and a relationship of trust, which is the first step to change.

HELP THEM FEEL A NEED TO CHANGE

Need is the element of change that is the primary precursor to action. Need is often called "the mother of change." No need . . . no change. People must have a need to change—meaning a deep-seated desire to change—if change is to take place in their lives. You might need to help someone see the need for change, and hopefully you will do it with love, agreed-upon values and goals, and common interests and concerns.

How can you create in someone else a need for wholesome change? In creating a need to change, you are often reaching out to a person who has varying degrees of readiness; a person may be self-sufficient or dependent, apathetic or energized, hateful or loving, frustrated or faithful. Your method of approach in creating the need for change varies from case to case. This is why motivation is so important as you create a climate for change through PIE.

Here are some guiding principles to help others feel the need to change:

- *Build enthusiasm for the desired outcome.* Excitement and enthusiasm are the flywheels of progress and growth.
- *Focus on rewards for excellent performance.* Receiving rewards for productive change is a basic dimension of a meaningful life. Sometimes you will need to design some tangible rewards, just as the Lord promises us blessings when we keep His commandments. With some people, on the other hand, the personal joy received from proper performance is sufficient.
- *Use joy in overcoming pain or discomfort as the catalyst for change.* When a person is in a situation that is painful, either physically or emotionally, this is an ideal time for change.
- *Take immediate action.* When the need is apparent and a person wants to change, that is the moment to act.

In summary, people tend to live according to the pattern of their current circumstances and environment. When they have needs or desires that are not fulfilled in their current circumstances, the thought of making changes is more acceptable. And when they receive praise, inspiration, and encouragement from a respected parent or friend, they are more willing to change.

HELP THEM FEEL INCREASED SELF-ESTEEM

There are many important days in a person's life; birthdays, anniversaries, personal victories, and a whole host of other grand moments are among the things that are traditionally celebrated. Yet other things of import are sometimes left in the shadows. *Who am I? What am I doing? Why am I here right now? Where am I going?* These questions linger in our minds but are often unaddressed or pushed aside for the "things" of the day that consume our time and usually end up controlling us rather than the other way around.

In order to feel truly good about themselves and understand their own worth, people need to know the following:

- They are loved.
- They are unique and special.
- They have talents and abilities that will enable them to achieve their goals.
- They have individual potential to do good and make contributions to other people's lives.
- They are the children of God with infinite worth.

Each one of those bulleted items is true—sometimes in varying degrees but always true.

People have eyes to see and hearts to feel, and they have the power within them to act accordingly. They are special. They are of worth. They can do many things of their own free will. Self-esteem and self-worth are vital to the empowerment of those we seek to help.

HOW TO BUILD SELF-ESTEEM IN OTHERS

Consider the following five suggestions:

1. Give Genuine Praise and Encouragement

If you are alert to opportunities to praise others, you will lift those people. But if that's to happen, the praise must be genuine.

Like many families, we held regular family home evening. We usually had a lesson on being good, discussed the calendar of what was happening in our family so all could support each other, and played games or had a special activity. We usually wrapped it all up with dessert. It was great fun.

Once a month, I had each child come up in front of the family, and I told everyone how great this child was and something this child had done that was so wonderful. On this particular night, it was Cory's turn. Cory was five years old, and I had mentioned to my sweetheart that I didn't have anything special to say about Cory. She reminded me that Cory put the dishes away after breakfast and consistently did a wonderful job.

So, with Cory by my side and my arm around him, I said, "Kids, your little brother Cory Matthew Pinegar is the greatest dish-putter-awayer in the whole world." A big smile came across Cory's face. I gave him a hug, and all the other kids cheered.

The results were amazing. The following week, Cory rushed around bringing the dishes to the sink and asking his mother, "Is that perfect?" She complimented him, thanked him, and encouraged him in his assignment.

At the end of that week, my sweetheart said to me, "If you thought he was doing a good job before, you should see him now. His work before doesn't even compare to what he's doing now. He is absolutely the greatest."

Why did Cory improve so much? Because that little boy was praised and encouraged to do his work. All it took was a little sliver of PIE. This kind of praise is miraculous. It is powerful. It is a forgotten virtue of change. Praise your children and all those with whom you work.

2. Help People Recognize Who They Really Are and All They Can Do

Parents and teachers especially have the precious responsibility of instilling within the hearts of children at the earliest stages that they are capable and loved. Each child has a promise of potential and the promise to achieve success. Each has an earthly mission of worth to perform. Children need to be taught purpose in life, appreciation of life itself, and thankfulness for their gifts and good qualities as they unfold through the years.

That's not just true for children. It applies to people of all ages. Everyone needs to know that they can do wonderful and helpful things that bless others and bring joy to their lives.

3. Give Responsibility and Require Accountability

There is no growth where there is no responsibility given or accountability required. The title, the job, the role—whatever it is—gives rise to performance according to the degree to which one accepts responsibility. Great people are made from great situations—and normal people become great people when they deal with situations in a great way. When given responsibility and accountability, people come to realize all the things they can accomplish.

4. Help Them Have a Successful Experience

Everyone needs a successful experience. Success breeds more success. You can provide opportunities for those experiences by knowing the abilities and desires of those with whom you work and then programming events or assignments within the capabilities of those you are trying to lift.

There are many meaningful activities, including the arts, athletics, educational pursuits, entrepreneurial tasks, and service projects, to name a few, in which people can find a niche for success and feel useful. The praising and inspirational moments will help them grow, become better, and do better. Your encouragement along the way is vital to the process of successful experiences.

This is especially important for people in coming to a knowledge of the truth in the scriptures and seeing the value of the word of God in their lives. Daily time with the Book of Mormon is vital to stay on the covenant path. People who feast upon the words of Christ and hold fast to the iron rod eventually arrive at the tree of life and partake of the love of God.

5. Enlist Peers in the Effort

As people grow, peer approval is incredibly important. You can enlist the help of a peer to find ways of building self-esteem in one who is temporarily suffering from a feeling of inadequacy. To be accepted by a colleague or praised by a friend is often the impetus for further growth.

My friend had a teenager who was struggling mightily with self-esteem. It's a harsh world out there these days for our teens, and they need all the boosts to their self-esteem they can get! This mom had confided her concerns about her son to one of her dear friends who had teens of her own. That friend began dropping off anonymous little treats and notes for the struggling teen—short messages like "You are awesome!" or "We think you are the coolest!" He had no idea who was leaving the items, but there was an immediate and visible change in his demeanor. Someone thought he was awesome enough to go to the effort to leave him surprises on his doorstep! To this day he has no idea who the "secret admirer" was, and his mom will never tell, but she is very grateful that someone enlisted to help strengthen her son's self-esteem at a critical time in his life.

When individuals truly become aware of their noble being and of the worth of their soul—when they realize that they are loved and have great potential—they begin to understand life and its precious value. The decision to change can then be made, and meaningful progress begins to happen. It is not something that happens all at once, but rather, it is a process of becoming. It is gradual, little by little, line upon line, as our understanding and increasing capacities permit.

GIVE THEM INFORMATION TO ACT ON AND SPECIFIC THINGS TO DO

With respect, need, and self-esteem in place, people can begin to act in accordance with their goals and plans to do specific things. Strength and success come to them in their efforts to change when they go from distant and general goals to specific, immediate action. A vague self-promise to improve does not work nearly as well as a commitment made with another person, especially one with a follow-up date for evaluation and review. A daily roster of "specific things to do today" will inevitably bring better results than an undirected day of taking what comes and moving as the mood dictates.

An abstract objective, such as "I'm going to lose weight," is not likely to bring as much success as a specific plan of action, such as "I am going to lose three pounds this month by cutting sugar and soda pop out of my diet." If someone says, "I should clean up the yard," that day might come—but isn't it more possible that the yard will get cleaned if one attacks the project directly by saying, "I'll pull the weeds today"?

One of the fundamental secrets of change is to obtain essential information relating to a person's goals—the facts and principles that belong to a specific course of action— and then act on these facts and principles in order to reap the blessings. Here is a checklist of indispensable questions to have them ask themselves as they set their goals:

- *What matters most in my life?*
- *What are my standards and values?*
- *What do I want to have happen?*
- *What needs to be done today? This week? This month?*
- *What are my goals and plans and how should they be prioritized?*
- *Do I have the information I need to achieve my goals and implement my plans?*

Get the facts! Involve your group or family and work together where required or expected. Make a plan with specific, achievable action items. With a few small wins, the necessary confidence can be gained to stay the course and accomplish big goals!

THE POWER TO CHANGE

When considering what you need to do to help others change, remember the following principles in your relationships and service:

- Act with love and a commitment to serve them through genuine acts of PIE throughout the change and growth experience.
- Relate to their level of understanding according to *where they are now* in their progress.
- Show strong enthusiasm for them.
- Act with conviction concerning their enduring values.
- Be realistic and down-to-earth with their plan for their everyday life.

- Be credible through your knowledge and through showing your desire to help them.
- Understand their needs, interests, and problems.
- Use all these principles of change to foster their commitment to follow your counsel.

HELP THEM CREATE THEIR VALUE SYSTEM

When you are trying to help people make changes, help them cultivate a value system. Identifying a solid value system is a blessing with lasting ramifications and will determine to a large extent their destiny in life and what they will accomplish.

Consider the definition of *value*: "relative worth, utility, or importance."[3] Other reference sources indicate that value is precious, beyond price, important, significant, superior, and something to prize and esteem.

What, then, do the people you are trying to help value? What is of most worth to them today? What is of most worth to them eternally? What spiritual values do they treasure? What temporal things do they value? What are they willing to do to preserve their values?

To create a lasting value system, they need to be willing to pass through a new kind of gateway—the covenant path, one leading onto the straight and narrow path where one is easily entreated and willing to follow our Savior Jesus Christ. Remember, "The Lord requireth the heart and a willing mind."[4] Moving along this pathway requires meekness, lowliness, and a demonstration of our humility as we understand our relationship to God and our dependence on Him. Holding fast to the iron rod requires respecting and

---

3   "Value," *Merriam-Webster.com*, 2021, https://www.merriam-webster.com/dictionary/value (February 4, 2021).
4   D&C 64:34.

loving others, discerning needs that can bring new possibilities for change, cultivating self-esteem, confirming true principles, applying those principles to their lives, and honoring their commitments. Traveling along this new kind of pathway toward lasting happiness also takes courage—courage to be realistic by applying values and knowledge productively. Following Christ and the values of His gospel is the only way people truly change.

Everyone values happiness—true, long-lasting happiness. No one gains true happiness through immediate self-aggrandizement to satisfy inclinations and appetites. Success and happiness come to people only from knowing their values, their motivations, the rules they will live by, the point beyond which they will not step in a time of crisis or temptation, and pinpointing the principles that motivate them and influence their decisions.

The values in the gospel of Jesus Christ can lead the people you are helping to happiness. In King Benjamin's sermon, he said:

> I would desire that ye should consider on the blessed and happy state of those that keep the commandments of God. For behold, they are blessed in all things, both temporal and spiritual; and if they hold out faithful to the end they are received into heaven, that thereby they may dwell with God in a state of never-ending happiness. O remember, remember that these things are true; for the Lord God hath spoken it.[5]

5　Mosiah 2:41.

Such self-examination will help people determine whether they are living the commandments of God. Being true to their values and living the commandments will keep them on the covenant path.

Most problems in interpersonal relationships and communication between people in relationships occur because of differing value systems. Even within the gospel of Jesus Christ, everyone has his or her own value system that is based on everything they have heard, seen, felt, experienced, or sought to enjoy. Other factors influencing a value system are a person's secret desires, frustrations, or things he or she has been exposed to in life. This is why the admonition to teach children early is so important—so they can begin to set up their criteria on how to judge righteously by the power of the Holy Spirit.[6]

The ideal toward which you can work is a progressive approach to value the gospel of Jesus Christ, which is based on eternal principles and truths. When at last people are truly touched by the Holy Spirit regarding the principles involved or the plan devised, their values are solidified. They are then in an authentic state of preparedness to change, to live in a new Christlike way "after the manner of happiness."[7]

Help people understand that their values eventually come out in their actions and their ways of life. When they value the word of God and the knowledge of truth, they will become directed by the Holy Spirit in their lives.

HELP THEM SUSTAIN THEIR COMMITMENT TO CHANGE

Your commitment to help others—to give them PIE on a regular basis—will help them stay committed to their

---

6 See D&C 11:12.

7 2 Nephi 5:27.

goals and the changes they need to make in their lives. Do they understand what it means to be committed to improve and change? Does *change* mean simply to accept a new idea? Does it mean to change one's views to conform to a pattern of behavior that was not embraced before certain truths came into one's life? What does it require?

HOW DOES ONE BECOME COMMITTED?

You can help people start on the path of dedication, obedience, study, and self-mastery—the covenant path. That means they come to understand and appreciate the word of God, their view of themselves, and how to improve.

The principles of change are the procedures that help them *stay* on the covenant path. That is why we make covenants with Heavenly Father and our Savior. Every principle of change follows the eternal truths that will help us become like Christ. Using PIE will help you assist others along their path to eternal life.

Establishing a pattern of commitment that will move people toward true transformation gives them faith and a positive attitude that they can change. They can change the outcomes of the past according to their new understanding and value system. They can embrace a commitment to themselves and others. And they can act so as to make that commitment a governing aspect of their lives.

AN ILLUSTRATION OF COMMITMENT

Commitments can be made at all ages and in all things. I remember how my son Steven made such a commitment. Steve came to me the Monday following a basketball tournament and said, "Dad, I've simply got to work harder."

I wished to help him and responded with an idea. "Why don't you start getting up at six a.m. and playing basketball before school?"

So in the middle of March, after basketball season was over, Steve began again—up every morning at six a.m., doing the drills, shooting the baskets, jumping rope, running. One night during family home evening, Steve said, "Say, Dad, you used to get up with me in the morning; why not get up with me now? How about on Tuesday morning at six a.m.?"

Being a converted father, I said, "I'll be up."

Tuesday morning when the alarm went off at six a.m., I looked out the window and what did I see? Popcorn popping on one apricot tree, and . . . it was snowing! I figured if it was snowing, we couldn't do anything outside, and I could go back to sleep. I climbed carefully back into bed. Then, in the very still of the morning, I could hear a little tiny noise as the basketball hit the rim and echoed through the house. You could only hear it if you were trying to go to sleep. I thought to myself, *If Steve can get up, I can get up.*

I quickly put on my gym clothes and my warm-up suit and went outside. And there, in the driveway, stood my son—a sixteen-year-old boy in two inches of snow, hands red as can be, shooting the basketball. He looked at me and grinned. "A few more, and I'll have my hundred shots in." I rebounded for him a little longer, then we went inside.

True to himself, he had made a commitment to get up at six a.m. to play basketball every day, and he did. It was a commitment.

You should make this same commitment—not necessarily to play basketball, though it is a good sport to play—but the commitment that you will do things for the improvement of yourself and others, that you will be committed to do your best and to be a good example at all times. When you are committed to change, you cannot help but encourage others to make the same commitment. Whenever you create an opportunity for someone to make a commitment, you should do everything possible to support and encourage that person.

You make these life-changing commitments with the Lord through receiving the ordinances and covenants of the gospel. You come with a broken heart and a contrite spirit, in a repentant posture with godly sorrow, to renew your covenants and commandments on a weekly basis by partaking of the sacrament. This covenant process is the way the Lord helps you keep your commitments.

Following is an action list that might help you assist others in becoming more committed to worthy endeavors:

- Use all the principles of change you've learned so far and respect them; help them feel a need to change; help them increase their self-esteem; help them understand the specific information to act on; help them identify their value system; and sustain them in their commitment.
- Express love to them. Reinforce them with genuine praise, inspiration, and continual encouragement.
- Recognize that those making the change need to personally make the decision in order to keep the commitment.
- Act with faith and prayers on their behalf.
- Show them the fruits of commitment, thus sustaining them during the process of change.
- Help them establish attainable goals that they can commit to.

- Continually confirm the necessity of self-mastery and self-discipline; commitment then becomes a byproduct.
- Help them accept support from others besides themselves—especially from Heavenly Father. Be a helper, not a judge.
- Always seek to inspire them with the word of God and encourage them along the way.

REMEMBER

Now is the time to help others achieve their goals and make some changes in their lives. When you are converted to making positive change, you cannot help but turn to others with a desire for them to have that same joy of self-fulfillment and service.

Every day you encounter opportunities to help those around you. Every day you come upon choices to act for the good of yourself and others. How do you respond to such opportunities? How do you ensure that you choose the higher road and take the steps to praise, inspire, and encourage those who need your help? In other words, how do you choose to make PIE a central part of your relationships and service?

You make the changes necessary to think of ways to praise, inspire, and encourage everyone you can. This is a mindset. What you think about will eventually become who you are. Consider the "thought process":

- A *thought* (perceived or received) is an idea, a consideration, a reflection, a deliberation, a concept, an aspiration, a meditation, or a pondering. When this "thought" is . . .
- Dwelled upon—that is, continually present in your mind such that you are engrossed in it and linger on it—this, in turn . . .

- Creates a desire—a want, a need, a penchant, a wish, a willingness, a longing, an appetite, a passion, or a craving for something. When this is . . .

- Encouraged—which is to urge, help, inspire, promote, support, motivate, stimulate, strengthen, and reassure— then it . . .

- Results in action—which is to perform, execute, give effort, and exert oneself. You actually do something. Your attitude has changed, and you now behave in a new way. You are a result of your thoughts, which, if they are righteous and principle-centered, always lead to . . .

- Benefits and positive consequences—the desirable outcomes of wise and prudent thinking and action.

The process for the transition from thoughts to desire to action is enhanced as you understand the principles of change and the associated blessings that come with a charitable heart and the practice of blessing others. The question, at that point, is one of initiative and self-mastery: Will you, in fact, remember? Will you think of others and how you can lift and inspire them? Remember, the key point in changing your life is to change your thought pattern. "For as he thinketh in his heart, so is he."[8]

---

8 Proverbs 23:7.

Chapter 6
GETTING SERIOUS ABOUT PIE

Do Heavenly Father and our Savior Jesus Christ praise, inspire, and encourage us?

YES!

Understanding the ways in which the Father, the Savior, and the Holy Ghost praise, inspire, and encourage us can help us understand ways in which we can do the same for those we want to help.

HOW DOES THE LORD PRAISE HIS PEOPLE?

The Lord's praise is always genuine and is used when one is deserving of praise. When introducing His Beloved Son Jesus Christ, Heavenly Father always includes a phrase saying how pleased He is with His Son. One example was when the Father introduced His Son to the Nephites in Bountiful: "Behold my Beloved Son, in whom I am well pleased, in whom I have glorified my name—hear ye him."[1]

Pleasing God was our Savior's constant desire:

> Then said Jesus unto them, When ye have
> lifted up the Son of man, then shall ye know

1   3 Nephi 11:7.

that I am he, and that I do nothing of myself;
but as my Father hath taught me, I speak these
things.

And he that sent me is with me: *the
Father hath not left me alone*; for I do always
those things that please him.[2]

God the Father taught and inspired His Son. God was with
His Son to encourage Him in all that He did.[3]

God is a God of love. When we love others, "God dwelleth
in us":

Beloved, let us love one another: for love is
of God; and every one that loveth is born
of God, and knoweth God.

He that loveth not knoweth not God;
for God is love.

In this was manifested the love of God
toward us, because that God sent his only
begotten Son into the world, that we might
live through him.

Herein is love, not that we loved God,
but that he loved us, and sent his Son to be
the propitiation for our sins.

Beloved, if God so loved us, we ought
also to love one another.

No man hath seen God at any time. If
we love one another, God dwelleth in us, and
his love is perfected in us.

---

2   John 8:28–29; emphasis added.
3   See Acts 10:38.

> Hereby know we that we dwell in him,
> and he in us, because he hath given us of his
> Spirit.[4]

Remember that praise, inspiration, and encouragement of others are expressions of love.

The Lord also offers rich examples of ways to praise, inspire, and encourage. I encourage you to read and ponder the following examples of the Lord giving PIE to his servants:

- 1 Nephi 2:1–2, in which He praises Lehi and inspires him to act.
- 1 Nephi 2:19–20, where He provides praise and inspiration to Nephi[5].
- Enos 1:5, 27, where He inspires Enos.
- Mosiah 26:15, which is filled with praise and encouragement for Alma the Elder.
- Alma 8:15, in which the Lord gives PIE to Alma the Younger.
- Helaman 10:4–5, where He praises, encourages, and inspires Nephi, the son of Helaman.

Many more examples are found throughout the scriptures. The Lord and His messengers are complimentary to all of His faithful servants.

The Lord is continually reaching out to you and all of us to inspire us to carry on and to encourage us to do better and be better. In counseling His prophets, the Lord reminded them to continually work with the struggling and unrepentant souls:

> Nevertheless, ye shall not cast him out from
> among you, but ye shall minister unto him

---

4   1 John 4:7–13.
5   See also 1 Nephi 11:6.

and shall pray for him unto the Father, in my name; and if it so be that he repenteth and is baptized in my name, then shall ye receive him, and shall minister unto him of my flesh and blood.

But if he repent not he shall not be numbered among my people, that he may not destroy my people, for behold I know my sheep, and they are numbered.

Nevertheless, ye shall not cast him out of your synagogues, or your places of worship, for unto such shall ye continue to minister; for ye know not but what they will return and repent, and come unto me with full purpose of heart, and I shall heal them; and ye shall be the means of bringing salvation unto them.

Therefore, keep these sayings which I have commanded you that ye come not under condemnation; for wo unto him whom the Father condemneth.[6]

The Lord expects you and all of us to keep ministering to the wayward, else we stand under condemnation.

The prophets are always recognizing their weaknesses and imperfections. That's because they are meek and lowly and full of humility. Why? Because they not only know their relationship to God as one of His sons, but they are totally dependent upon His grace and goodness so that they might succeed as a messenger and prophet of God.

---

6   3 Nephi 18:30–33.

Moses and Enoch were both reluctant to serve, yet the Lord always inspired them and encouraged them by reminding them that He would support and sustain them.

Look at the example of Moses:

> And Moses said unto the Lord, *O my Lord, I am not eloquent, neither heretofore, nor since thou hast spoken unto thy servant: but I am slow of speech, and of a slow tongue.*
>
> And the Lord said unto him, Who hath made man's mouth? or who maketh the dumb, or deaf, or the seeing, or the blind? have not I the Lord?
>
> Now therefore go, and I will be with thy mouth, and teach thee what thou shalt say.[7]

And from the book of Moses, we learn: "And it came to pass that it was for the space of many hours before Moses did again receive his natural strength like unto man; and he said unto himself: Now, *for this cause I know that man is nothing, which thing I never had supposed.*"[8]

Enoch's experience with the Lord in Moses 6:27–39 also gives remarkable insight into the way the Lord praises, inspires, and encourages His people.

In addition to the examples of Heavenly Father inspiring and encouraging His people, it's clear that God also chastises His prophets and His people. Why? Because He loves us with a complete and perfect love, and He seeks to help us on our way and keep us on the covenant path. Chastening is actually

---

7 Exodus 4:10–12; emphasis added.
8 Moses 1:10; emphasis added.

a way to inspire all of us to be better and do better according to the will of God:

> And ye have forgotten the exhortation which speaketh unto you as unto children, My son, despise not thou the chastening of the Lord, nor faint when thou art rebuked of him.
>
> For whom the Lord loveth he chasteneth, and scourgeth every son whom he receiveth.
>
> If ye endure chastening, God dealeth with you as with sons; for what son is he whom the father chasteneth not?[9]

HOW DOES THE LORD INSPIRE HIS PEOPLE?

The ability to influence or be influenced is part of what is called *inspiration and motivation*. Inspirational and motivational power affects the mind and heart, the very seat of the spirit within our very being. The Lord has said:

> Oliver Cowdery, verily, verily, I say unto you, that assuredly as the Lord liveth, who is your God and your Redeemer, even so surely shall you receive a knowledge of whatsoever things you shall ask in faith, with an honest heart, believing that you shall receive a knowledge concerning the engravings of old records, which are ancient, which contain those parts of my scripture of which has been spoken by the manifestation of my Spirit.
>
> Yea, behold, I will tell you in your mind and in your heart, by the Holy Ghost, which

---

9   Hebrews 12:5-7; see also verses 8-14.

shall come upon you and which shall dwell in your heart.

Now, behold, this is the spirit of revelation; behold, this is the spirit by which Moses brought the children of Israel through the Red Sea on dry ground.[10]

Responding to that power, we become excited, enlivened, and even provoked to greater heights. It truly prompts us to be better. This phenomenon is a result of our reaction to any given experience. The effect depends on the attitudes of both the giver and the receiver of the information and the conditions at the moment. When one feels a need for something, the power to be inspired is greatly enhanced. You should be constantly looking for ways to inspire and motivate those you are trying to help.

Heavenly Father loved all of us so much that He gave His Beloved Son Jesus Christ.[11] The Lord's Atonement inspires us all in all things and draws us unto the Lord.[12] The Lord's Atonement is the foundation of all faith, hope, joy, peace, forgiveness, and redemption. It is the Balm of Gilead, the renewing essence of the gospel. It is the key to everlasting life. It is the essence of our promise of obedience to the Lord. It is the victory over death, the binding covenant of love. It is the key for coming to know Deity as the Author of life eternal. The Lord's Atonement is the empowerment of everlasting "oneness" with our Father and His Son. Through the Lord's Atonement, we are nurtured and succored according to our afflictions and tribulations.[13]

---

10   D&C 8:1–3.
11   See John 3:16.
12   See 3 Nephi 27:13–17.
13   See Alma 7:11–12.

We are drawn to the Lord by His Atonement. "And my Father sent me that I might be lifted up upon the cross; and after that I had been lifted up upon the cross, that I might draw all men unto me."[14]

THE INSPIRING POWER OF SACRIFICE

The Lord's Atonement is the ultimate example of sacrifice. Sacrifice is an exalting principle because it flows outward from an inner reservoir of love and obedience. Sacrifice requires humility and great love. Those who witness your sacrifice for others will be able to see and understand the truths behind it and be inspired because of your meekness and willingness to give.

Consider these memorable passages of scripture concerning sacrifice:

- Psalm 51:17: "The sacrifices of God are a broken spirit: a broken and a contrite heart, O God, thou wilt not despise."[15]
- John 15:13: "Greater love hath no man than this, that a man lay down his life for his friends."
- 2 Nephi 2:7: "Behold, he (our Savior Jesus Christ) offereth himself a sacrifice for sin, to answer the ends of the law, unto all those who have a broken heart and a contrite spirit; and unto none else can the ends of the law be answered."
- Alma 34:14–16: "And behold, this is the whole meaning of the law, every whit pointing to that great and last sacrifice; and that great and last sacrifice will be the Son of God, yea, infinite and eternal. And thus he shall bring salvation to all those who shall believe on his name; this being the intent of this last sacrifice, to bring about

---

14   3 Nephi 27:14.
15   See also 3 Nephi 9:20.

the bowels of mercy, which overpowereth justice, and bringeth about means unto men that they may have faith unto repentance. And thus mercy can satisfy the demands of justice, and encircles them in the arms of safety, while he that exercises no faith unto repentance is exposed to the whole law of the demands of justice; therefore only unto him that has faith unto repentance is brought about the great and eternal plan of redemption."

- 3 Nephi 9:20: "And ye shall offer for a sacrifice unto me a broken heart and a contrite spirit. And whoso cometh unto me with a broken heart and a contrite spirit, him will I baptize with fire and with the Holy Ghost, even as the Lamanites, because of their faith in me at the time of their conversion, were baptized with fire and with the Holy Ghost, and they knew it not."

- D&C 97:8–9: "Verily I say unto you, all among them who know their hearts are honest, and are broken, and their spirits contrite, and are willing to observe their covenants by sacrifice—yea, every sacrifice which I, the Lord, shall command—they are accepted of me. For I, the Lord, will cause them to bring forth as a very fruitful tree which is planted in a goodly land, by a pure stream, that yieldeth much precious fruit."

The eternal Exemplar of sacrifice is Jesus Christ, who gave His life for the immortality and eternal life of man. Throughout all dispensations of time, the Lord has required His children to make sacrifice an indispensable dimension of daily living as a constant reminder of the mercy and grace embodied in His own atoning sacrifice on our behalf.

Each faithful son or daughter of God is imbued with the spirit of charity toward all and the faithful commitment

to sacrifice all that is required for the building up of the
kingdom of God. "Thou shalt offer a sacrifice unto the Lord
thy God in righteousness, even that of a broken heart and a
contrite spirit."[16] You can preserve and share with others your
inspiration and experiences about the sacred blessings that
flow from sacrifice and obedience.

Remember, great blessings flow from making choices in
favor of the Lord, which often require sacrifice and which
always require obedience. The opportunity to participate
actively in building up the kingdom of God is the pearl of
great price—not to be exchanged for any professional pursuit:
"But seek ye first the kingdom of God and his righteousness,
and all these things shall be added unto you."[17]

THE INSPIRING POWER OF THE WORD OF GOD

The scriptures are perfect examples of being inspired
by the power of the word of God. Consider the following:
"But there is a spirit in man: and the inspiration of the
Almighty giveth them understanding."[18]

There is in us a spirit that can communicate with and be
inspired by the Spirit of God. Indeed, through the gift of the
Holy Ghost, a "portion of that spirit" dwells in us.[19] Heavenly
Father, through the Holy Spirit, gives us understanding.
Understanding brings appreciation and gratitude, which will
inspire us to change in both attitude and behavior: "But the
Comforter, which is the Holy Ghost, whom the Father will
send in my name, he shall teach you all things, and bring all

---

16   D&C 59:8.
17   3 Nephi 13:33; compare Matthew 6:33.
18   Job 32:8.
19   Alma 18:35.

things to your remembrance, whatsoever I have said unto you."[20] We can and will be inspired by the teachings of the Spirit.[21]

It is always the Spirit that will move us to action through faith in the Lord Jesus Christ: "And I was led by the Spirit, not knowing beforehand the things which I should do."[22] When we live worthy of the Spirit, we can always depend on it to direct our lives. It will show us the things to do[23] and give us the things to say.[24]

> And I know that the Lord God will consecrate my prayers for the gain of my people. And the words which I have written in weakness will be made strong unto them; for it persuadeth them to do good; it maketh known unto them of their fathers; and it speaketh of Jesus, and persuadeth them to believe in him, and to endure to the end, which is life eternal.[25]

The word of God has power to motivate and inspire us to do good.[26] It can, if we give place for it in our hearts, change us forever. We should live by every word that proceedeth from the mouth of God.[27]

> Now, it came to pass that when I had heard these words I began to feel a desire for the welfare of my brethren, the Nephites;

20 John 14:26.
21 See Galatians 5:22–23; D&C 11:12–13.
22 1 Nephi 4:6.
23 See 2 Nephi 32:5.
24 See D&C 100:5–6.
25 2 Nephi 33:4.
26 See Alma 31:5.
27 See D&C 84:44–46.

> wherefore, I did pour out my whole soul
> unto God for them.[28]

When Enos received a remission of his sins through faith on the Lord, he was motivated and inspired to do good. He had concern for the welfare of his fellowmen. When our faith increases, we too will have been inspired to do good continually:

> And they all cried with one voice, saying:
> Yea, we believe all the words which thou hast
> spoken unto us; and also, we know of their
> surety and truth, because of the Spirit of
> the Lord Omnipotent, which has wrought
> a mighty change in us, or in our hearts, that
> we have no more disposition to do evil, but
> to do good continually.[29]

Conversion—the mighty change of heart, the process of being born again—brings a power within that comes from God by the power of the Holy Ghost. The people of King Benjamin had that experience, and so can we. When we truly change, we will not only be motivated to be good, but we will want to inspire others to do so as well.[30]

The things of God have the power to inspire us as we yield to the enticings of the Holy Spirit. We will be Saints of the Most High God. We will be submissive to His will and keep the commandments.[31]

---

28 Enos 1:9.
29 Mosiah 5:2.
30 See Mosiah 28:3.
31 See Mosiah 3:19.

> Verily, verily, I say unto you, I will impart
> unto you of my Spirit, which shall enlighten
> your mind, which shall fill your soul with
> joy.[32]

The Holy Spirit opens our minds to the things of the Lord. We will have desires to do good, walk humbly, do justly, and judge righteously.[33]

The scriptures—the word of God—are like inspirational letters from our Heavenly Father and our Savior Jesus Christ constantly before us to feast upon daily so we can stay on the straight and narrow path, the covenant path, which leads to eternal life. Nephi admonished us to feast upon the word:

> Wherefore, ye must press forward with a
> steadfastness in Christ, having a perfect
> brightness of hope, and a love of God and of
> all men. Wherefore, *if ye shall press forward,
> feasting upon the word of Christ, and endure to
> the end, behold, thus saith the Father: Ye shall
> have eternal life.*[34]

How is the Book of Mormon a shield of protection and a "flaming fire"[35] of inspiration for our day?

Let's consider Moroni's title page for the Book of Mormon. As this prophet looked back over two and a half millennia of history and prepared to bury the records and the abridgement in the ground for a later generation, how did he summarize the essence of the Book of Mormon? He

32   D&C 11:13.
33   See D&C 11:12.
34   2 Nephi 31:20; emphasis added.
35   2 Nephi 14:5; compare Isaiah 4:5.

saw it as a shield of protection and a fountain of inspiration for our day. Moroni identified in his title page the four key dimensions of this inspiring scriptural enlightenment:

> Which is to show unto the remnant of the House of Israel what great things the Lord hath done for their fathers; and that they may know the covenants of the Lord, that they are not cast off forever—And also to the convincing of the Jew and Gentile that JESUS is the CHRIST, the ETERNAL GOD, manifesting himself unto all nations.

Thus, the agenda of the entire Book of Mormon can be summarized in four points:

1. To preserve and present great stories from the past concerning the Lord's loving mercy to His children. The tender mercies of God are all demonstrations of inspiration and encouragement to carry on.
2. To teach about great and sacred covenants that still apply in our day. The promised blessings are meant to encourage us to greater obedience and faithfulness.
3. To engender great hope for the future—in other words, that we are not "cast off forever" but belong to the fold of Christ forever. Hope is the overlying principle and doctrine of encouragement.
4. To build all of this upon the sure foundation of our Savior Jesus Christ, the great Redeemer.

This fourfold agenda is the key to the Book of Mormon's strength and vitality as a "marvelous work and a wonder"[36] gifted to us by the Lord for our day.

---

36   Isaiah 29:14; 2 Nephi 25:17; 27:26.

Our prophets have encouraged us to feast daily on the Book of Mormon. The Prophet Joseph Smith wrote in the introduction to the Book of Mormon, "I told the brethren that the Book of Mormon was the most correct of any book on earth, and the keystone of our religion, and a man would get nearer to God by abiding by its precepts, than by any other book." The message is clear: the book contains inspiring words for the Lord's people to live by—precepts that will bring us near to God, else we perish and wander off the covenant path into strange lands without direction and empowerment.

Let's look at a few of the many inspired treasures of truth preserved in the Book of Mormon:

- **Devotion**—from the words of Nephi: "I will go and do the things which the Lord hath commanded, for I know that the Lord giveth no commandments unto the children of men, save he shall prepare a way for them that they may accomplish the thing which he commandeth them."[37]

- **Faith**—in the example of the brother of Jared, who was so perfect in his belief that he saw the Lord: "Because of thy faith thou hast seen that I shall take upon me flesh and blood; and never has man come before me with such exceeding faith as thou hast; for were it not so ye could not have seen my finger."[38]

- **Revelation**—in the words of Moroni, concerning our reading of the Book of Mormon: "Ask God, the Eternal Father, in the name of Christ, if these things are not true; and if ye shall ask with a sincere heart, with real

---

37   1 Nephi 3:7.
38   Ether 3:9.

intent, having faith in Christ, he will manifest the truth of it unto you, by the power of the Holy Ghost. And by the power of the Holy Ghost ye may know the truth of all things."[39]

- **Savior as Redeemer**—from the words of Helaman: "And now, my sons, remember, remember that it is upon the rock of our Redeemer, who is Christ, the Son of God, that ye must build your foundation."[40]
- **Service**—from the words of King Benjamin: "And behold, I tell you these things that ye may learn wisdom; that ye may learn that when ye are in the service of your fellow beings ye are only in the service of your God."[41]
- **Witnessing**—from the words of Alma the Elder: "And to stand as witnesses of God at all times and in all things, and in all places that ye may be in, even until death, that ye may be redeemed of God, and be numbered with those of the first resurrection, that ye may have eternal life."[42]
- **Mercy and goodness of the Lord**—"Behold, I would exhort you that when ye shall read these things, if it be wisdom in God that ye should read them, that ye would remember how merciful the Lord hath been unto the children of men, from the creation of Adam even down until the time that ye shall receive these things, and ponder it in your hearts."[43]

All the above examples demonstrate the love of God and Christ. You are empowered through Their love with greater self-worth because of the expectations through Their

39   Moroni 10:4–5.
40   Helaman 5:12.
41   Mosiah 2:17.
42   Mosiah 18:9.
43   Moroni 10:3.

praise, inspiration, and encouragement. Great expectations come from trusting you with great responsibility.

The Lord's word is empowering. When you rely on it, there is a greater chance for change in the lives of people you are seeking to bless.[44]

The Lord was very adamant about living by the word of God when He said:

> *And I now give unto you a commandment to beware concerning yourselves, to give diligent heed to the words of eternal life.*
>
> *For you shall live by every word that proceedeth forth from the mouth of God.*
>
> For the word of the Lord is truth, and whatsoever is truth is light, and whatsoever is light is Spirit, even the Spirit of Jesus Christ.
>
> And the Spirit giveth light to every man that cometh into the world; and the Spirit enlighteneth every man through the world, that hearkeneth to the voice of the Spirit.
>
> And every one that hearkeneth to the voice of the Spirit cometh unto God, even the Father.[45]

HIS PROPHETS BRING MESSAGES FROM GOD TO HIS CHILDREN

Study Amos 3:7, D&C 1:38, and D&C 21:4–6. Ponder the power and the meaning of these scriptures about how God uses His prophets to inspire His children.

---

44   See Alma 31:5.
45   D&C 84:43–47; emphasis added.

We have been given prophets, but that wasn't an idle gift. It is essential that we listen to them. Mormon issued a severe warning to those who do not give heed to the Lord's prophets:

> And wo be unto him that will not hearken unto the words of Jesus, and also to them whom he hath chosen and sent among them; for whoso receiveth not the words of Jesus and the words of those whom he hath sent receiveth not him; and therefore he will not receive them at the last day;
>
> And it would be better for them if they had not been born. For do ye suppose that ye can get rid of the justice of an offended God, who hath been trampled under feet of men, that thereby salvation might come?[46]

In the beginning of the Lord's sermon at the temple in Bountiful when He arrived in the Americas, He also said that it is vital to listen to the words of His prophets, promising that those who listened and believed would be blessed and receive a remission of their sins.[47]

The prophets sent by the Lord are sources of divine revelation, and that is no different in our day. You can more than listen to the revelation they receive; you can also qualify to receive your own revelation and inspiration. Consider a few of the things our modern-day prophets have shared about revelation and inspiration.

---

46 3 Nephi 28:34–35.

47 See 3 Nephi 12:1–2.

FROM GORDON B. HINCKLEY:

I am more concerned with the fact that God has revealed in this dispensation a great and marvelous and beautiful plan that motivates (inspires) men and women to love their Creator and their Redeemer, to appreciate and serve one another, to walk in faith on the road that leads to immortality and eternal life.[48]

FROM EZRA TAFT BENSON:

Inspiration comes from prayer.[49] Inspiration is essential to properly lead.[50] We must have the spirit of inspiration whether we are teaching[51] or administering the affairs of the kingdom.[52] If we do our part in preparation and work and have the Spirit of the Lord, we can be led, though we do not know beforehand what needs to be done.[53] Therefore, we should always pray, especially prior to commencing the work of the Lord.[54] [55]

---

48 *Faith: The Essence of True Religion* (Salt Lake City: Deseret Book, 1989), 17.

49 See D&C 63:64.

50 See D&C 50:13–14.

51 See D&C 50:13–14; Alma 17:3.

52 See D&C 46:2.

53 See 1 Nephi 4:6.

54 See 2 Nephi 32:9.

55 *The Teachings of Ezra Taft Benson* (Salt Lake City: Bookcraft, 1988), 433.

FROM THOMAS S. MONSON:

A patriarchal blessing is a revelation to the recipient, even a white line down the middle of the road, to protect, inspire, and motivate activity and righteousness.[56]

FROM MARVIN J. ASHTON:

Many people are motivated by spiritual goals. The question is, "For what reasons?" Is it because of good feelings and promised rewards, or is it because of fear of not living the commandments? The best motivation is toward the positive. Total commitment to correct gospel principles brings joy, satisfaction, and the abundant life.[57]

FROM RUSSELL M. NELSON:

The privilege of receiving revelation is one of the greatest gifts of God to His children.

Through the manifestations of the Holy Ghost, the Lord will assist us in all our righteous pursuits. . . .

I urge you to stretch beyond your current spiritual ability to receive personal revelation, for the Lord has promised that "if thou shalt (seek), thou shalt receive revelation upon revelation, knowledge upon knowledge, that thou mayest know the mysteries and peaceable things—that

56 *Live the Good Life* (Salt Lake City: Deseret Book, 1988), 38–39.
57 *Be of Good Cheer* (Salt Lake City: Deseret Book, 1987), 50.

which bringeth joy, that which bringeth life eternal."[58]

. . . But in coming days, it will not be possible to survive spiritually without the guiding, directing, comforting, and constant influence of the Holy Ghost.[59]

REMEMBER THE INSPIRING POWER OF THE LORD JESUS CHRIST AND THE HOLY GHOST

The Father, the Son, and the Holy Ghost inspire and encourage us along the only way back to the Father:

> And now, behold, my beloved brethren, this is the way; and there is none other way nor name given under heaven whereby man can be saved in the kingdom of God. And now, behold, this is the doctrine of Christ, and the only and true doctrine of the Father, and of the Son, and of the Holy Ghost, which is one God, without end. Amen.[60]

We have sacred assurance that the Lord is with us as we seek to build up the kingdom of God: "And whoso receiveth you, there I will be also, for I will go before your face. I will be on your right hand and on your left, and my Spirit shall be in your hearts, and mine angels round about you, to bear you up."[61]

Sacred words of eternal truth are given to us through the Father, His Son Jesus Christ, His messengers (angels and

---

58   D&C 42:61.

59   "Revelation for the Church, Revelation for Our Lives," *Ensign*, May 2018.

60   2 Nephi 31:21.

61   D&C 84:88.

prophets), and by the supernal power of the Holy Ghost. The words of Christ will tell us all things to do.[62] And because we believe in His Beloved Son, Heavenly Father gave us the gift and power of the Holy Ghost,[63] which will also show us all things to do.[64] The Holy Spirit "leadeth (us) to do good— yea, to do justly, to walk humbly, to judge righteously; and this is my Spirit. Verily, verily, I say unto you, I will impart unto you of my Spirit, which shall enlighten your mind, which shall fill your soul with joy."[65]

As we seek our Heavenly Father through prayer and fasting, we will be blessed according to our faith and needs. As we come unto Christ and follow Him, He will lead us along the pathway of redemption, for He is our Good Shepherd. The Holy Ghost will teach us, guide us, prompt us, and inspire us in all things. Elder James E. Talmage and Elder Parley P. Pratt spoke to the supernal nature and power of the Holy Ghost. Elder James E. Talmage taught:

> The Holy Ghost undoubtedly possesses personal powers and affections; these attributes exist in Him in perfection. Thus, He teaches and guides, testifies of the Father and the Son, reproves for sin, speaks, commands, and commissions, makes intercession for sinners, is grieved, searches and investigates, entices, and knows all things. These are not figurative expressions,

---

62 See 2 Nephi 32:3.
63 See 3 Nephi 9:20.
64 See 2 Nephi 32:5.
65 D&C 11:12–13.

but plain statements of the attributes and characteristics of the Holy Ghost.[66]

Elder Parley P. Pratt said this concerning the Holy Ghost:

The gift of the Holy Ghost . . . quickens all the intellectual faculties, increases, enlarges, expands and purifies all the natural passions and affections; and adapts them, by the gift of wisdom, to their lawful use. It inspires, develops, cultivates and matures all the fine-toned sympathies, joys, tastes, kindred feelings and affections of our nature. It inspires virtue, kindness, goodness, tenderness, gentleness, and charity.[67]

The prophet Wilford Woodruff expressed his witness by declaring:

You may have the administration of angels, you may see many miracles; you may see many wonders in the earth; but I claim that the gift of the Holy Ghost is the greatest gift that can be bestowed upon man.[68]

The Holy Ghost is the Revelator and inspires us in all things. He is our guide and will motivate us to do the will of God.

---

66   *Articles of Faith*, 144.
67   Parley P. Pratt, *Key to the Science of Theology*, 9th ed. (1965), 101, quoted in L. Tom Perry, "'That Spirit Which Leadeth to Do Good,'" *Ensign*, May 1997.
68   *The Discourses of Wilford Woodruff*, ed. G. Homer Durham (Salt Lake City: Deseret Book, 1946), 5.

HOW DOES THE LORD ENCOURAGE HIS PEOPLE?

With *every* covenant and commandment revealed, the Lord encourages us with promised blessings if we are faithful! Look at some of those promises as contained in the Book of Mormon.

TO LEHI'S COLONY:

> Wherefore, I, Lehi, have obtained a promise, that inasmuch as those whom the Lord God shall bring out of the land of Jerusalem shall keep his commandments, they shall prosper upon the face of this land; and they shall be kept from all other nations, that they may possess this land unto themselves. And if it so be that they shall keep his commandments they shall be blessed upon the face of this land, and there shall be none to molest them, nor to take away the land of their inheritance; and they shall dwell safely forever.[69]

TO NEPHI:

> And I heard a voice from the Father, saying: Yea, the words of my Beloved are true and faithful. He that endureth to the end, the same shall be saved.[70]

KING BENJAMIN TAUGHT:

> And moreover, I would desire that ye should consider on the blessed and happy state of

---

69   2 Nephi 1:9; see also 2 Nephi 1:20; 4:4; Jarom 1:9; Omni 1:6; Mosiah 1:7; 2:22, 31; Alma 9:13; 36:1, 30; 37:13; 38:1; 48:25; 50:20; Helaman 3:20.
70   2 Nephi 31:15.

those that keep the commandments of God. For behold, they are blessed in all things, both temporal and spiritual; and if they hold out faithful to the end they are received into heaven, that thereby they may dwell with God in a state of never-ending happiness. O remember, remember that these things are true; for the Lord God hath spoken it.[71]

ALMA TO THE PEOPLE IN ZARAHEMLA:

And behold, he preached the word unto your fathers, and a mighty change was also wrought in their hearts, and they humbled themselves and put their trust in the true and living God. And behold, they were faithful until the end; therefore they were saved.[72]

MORONI TO HIS ARMY:

Now ye see that this is the true faith of God; yea, ye see that God will support, and keep, and preserve us, so long as we are faithful unto him, and unto our faith, and our religion; and never will the Lord suffer that we shall be destroyed except we should fall into transgression and deny our faith.[73]

The Lord also encourages us through promised blessings found in the Doctrine and Covenants: "And if thou art faithful

---

71   Mosiah 2:41.

72   Alma 5:13.

73   Alma 44:4.

in keeping my commandments, thou shalt be lifted up at the last day."[74]

Thus we see that praise, inspiration, and encouragement are used by Heavenly Father and our Savior Jesus Christ as expressions of Their love and to help us stay on the covenant path and receive the blessings of eternal life. In that sacred context, ponder the following statements about the power of praise, inspiration, and encouragement.

- **Praise.** Honest and genuine praise will lift, inspire, provide a sense of approval, and honor and confirm a person's worth and performance. Praise enhances the person's well-being and dispels doubt and fear. It builds confidence and gives hope to move forward. Praise gives impetus to do even better.
- **Inspiration.** Inspiration comes by the power of the Holy Ghost. He will help you teach eternal truths and help those you teach come to the knowledge of Christ and of the truth.[75] Inspiration generates gratitude, the catalyst for positive change. Inspiration is given through persuasion, gentleness, patience, kindness, and the utmost concern for the welfare of the individual.
- **Encouragement.** Encouragement is the sunshine that fosters positive change. You can give encouragement in a kind way to facilitate authentic accomplishment. Encouragement is the safety net for the achievement of success.

74 D&C 5:35; of the hundred or more similar scriptures, see also 6:13, 20, 37; 14:7, 11; 31:13.

75 See Alma 23:5–6.

Epilogue
WHAT ARE YOU GOING TO DO?

As we wrap up our discussion on PIE and the process of meaningful change, there is a final question: What are you going to do now?

It's simple to start:

1. Start at the beginning—with your family. Pray and ponder how you will give PIE in a genuine and sincere manner to each member of your family.

2. Look at each family member and seek a time, a place, and a way to praise, inspire, and encourage them. Don't give the whole load at once. Give small doses as prompted by the Holy Ghost and according to the needs of each one.

3. Listen carefully to their conversations so you will know their wants and desires in life.

4. Next, expand your reach. Look for ways to give PIE to others. Dish up a little at a time according to their needs and your observations.

5. Finally, give PIE randomly and spontaneously to everybody you can! The world needs more PIE!

Enjoy life. Live it to the fullest. Seek to bring joy and happiness to others. Remember that you have the potential to do good. You have the capacity within you to do many noble and helpful things of your own free will and choice. You can do it. You can bless others' lives a little every day. Remember that giving PIE is part of the second great commandment: "Thou shalt love thy neighbour as thyself. On these two commandments *hang all the law and the prophets*."[76]

The phrase *hang all the law and the prophets* refers to the Old Testament. The *law* consists of all that was written in the first five books of the Old Testament. The *prophets* describe the remaining books of the Old Testament, which were written by the prophets. Loving God and our fellow men are the essence of all the laws of God in holy writ. Within the two great commandments is the expression of the pure love of Christ.

Love is the highest form of motivation. Expressing love through praise, inspiration, and encouragement (PIE) will help you continually think of others and will help you be a kind and loving person. God will bless *you* in all things. Look for those blessings and His tender mercies, and you will praise God every day of your life!

Praising God is the most important kind of praise you can express. Genuine praise to God, in all its forms, is a way of demonstrating your love and gratitude for all things. Offering praise to your Heavenly Father is the best way to overcome melancholy or disappointment or to transcend the burdens that sometimes come with this mortal experience. As Nephi wrote, "Nevertheless, I did look unto my God, and I did praise

76 Matthew 22:39–40; emphasis added.

him all the day long; and I did not murmur against the Lord because of mine afflictions."[77]

And when things are good and going well, the Lord counsels us, "If thou art merry, praise the Lord with singing, with music, with dancing, and with a prayer of praise and thanksgiving."[78]

We can all sing for joy as Saints of God, echoing the sentiment of Nephi in his psalm:

> Yea, I know that God will give liberally to him that asketh. Yea, my God will give me, if I ask not amiss; therefore I will lift up my voice unto thee; yea, I will cry unto thee, my God, the rock of my righteousness. Behold, my voice shall forever ascend up unto thee, my rock and mine everlasting God. Amen.[79]

As we learn to give PIE to one another, I hope that we will be able to become more like our Father in Heaven and our Savior Jesus Christ, who generously give us praise, inspiration, and encouragement throughout our lives. I testify to you that by serving PIE to those around you each day, you will see a change in them and in yourself. Your lives will be blessed with greater joy, a greater closeness with the Spirit, and perhaps a greater closeness to each other as well. That's because PIE is an expression of love—the love we have for our Father and our Savior, the love we have for each other, and the love They have for us.

---

77 1 Nephi 18:16.

78 D&C 136:28.

79 2 Nephi 4:35.

We have each been called to serve and teach in some capacity—as parents, as missionaries, as Sunday school instructors, friends, siblings, and in many other roles. So when you find yourself faltering in these roles, when you struggle to connect with others, when you're lost about how to uplift them, or when you're uncertain about how to help them, follow this one rule: let them have PIE. For when we lead with love, all else will follow.

Ed Jolley Pinegar

FEBRUARY 12, 1935–AUGUST 18, 2020

ED JOLLEY PINEGAR PEACEFULLY PASSED away on August 18, 2020, with his sweetheart, Pat, by his side. He was born in Provo, Utah, on February 12, 1935, to James Emery Pinegar and Effie Jolley Pinegar. Ed will be remembered as a beloved husband, father, grandfather, and great-grandfather, and as a teacher, speaker, author, dentist, and friend. His life was filled with service—praising, inspiring, and encouraging (PIE) others with humor and love.

Ed was raised in Edgemont, Spanish Fork, and Provo, Utah. He graduated from BYU Elementary Training School and BY High School. He excelled in athletics playing football, basketball, baseball, and tennis. He attended BYU on a tennis and basketball scholarship playing for the legendary Coach Stan Watts. In 1956, he graduated from BYU with a degree in chemistry and mathematics. He married his college sweetheart, Patricia Peterson, on March 28, 1956, in the Salt Lake Temple. They recently celebrated their sixty-fourth wedding anniversary.

Ed attended dental school at the University of Southern California and graduated in 1961. While attending dental school, he taught early-morning seminary to high school students. He began his dental practice in Provo, Utah. After one year, he was asked to put his practice aside to serve as a captain in the United States Army between 1962 and 1964. Upon returning to Provo to restart his dental practice, he again taught early-morning seminary for three years and then taught the Book of Mormon, Gospel Principles and Practices, and other religion classes part-time at BYU for nineteen years. He retired in 2000 from the faculty at the Orem Institute of Religion at Utah Valley University in Orem, Utah.

Ed served in many capacities as a member of The Church of Jesus Christ of Latter-day Saints. He served as bishop (twice) and stake president. He also served with Pat as President of the England London South Mission (1985–88), President of the Provo Missionary Training Center (1988–90), full-time missionaries to the church historical sites in the Rochester New York Mission, and as President and Matron of the Manti Temple (2009–12). His last calling was as a greeter in the Suncrest 10th Ward. He was the author of over sixty books and audio recordings, many of which were on missionary work.

The joy of Ed's life was his family. He loved his sweetheart, Pat, an angel wife and mother. They are the parents of eight children: Karie Bushnell (Bruce), Steve Pinegar, Kelly Hagemeyer (Dale), Kristi Gubler (Ross), Brett Pinegar (Susan), Cory Pinegar (who preceded him in death in 1986), Traci Magleby (Hans), and Tricia Skousen (Jeff). He has thirty-eight grandchildren and thirty great-grandchildren with five on the way.